CCENT

Troubleshooting Guide

ICND1 100-105

55 Practical Troubleshooting Exercises to Prepare You for the ICND1 100-105 Exam and the Field

MATT DAY

This publication is not endorsed by, sponsored by, or affiliated with Cisco Systems, Inc., Cisco, Cisco Systems, CCENT, or CCNA. Cisco Systems, CCENT and CCNA are registered trademarks of Cisco Systems, Inc. All other trademarks are property of their respective owners.

Legal Notice
The publisher and author make no representations or warranties with respect to the accuracy or completeness of the contents of this work and disclaim all warranties for any particular purpose. Although the author has made every effort to ensure that the information in this publication was correct at press time, the publisher and author do not assume and hereby disclaim any liability to any party for any loss, damage or disruption caused by errors or omissions. The advice, exercises and strategies in this book have been designed to assist you in preparing for the Cisco CCENT or CCNA certification exams and are intended to illustrate a technical point only. They are not suggested configurations and should not be applied to a production network. This work is sold with the understanding that the publisher and author are not engaged in rendering legal or other professional services. Neither the publisher nor the author shall be liable for damages arising herefrom.

Updates/Errata
If errors are discovered in this publication after press time, updates and errata sheets will be made available at www.SkillsClimber.com/CCENTTroubleshootingGuide.

About the Author
Matt Day is a Cisco Certified Network Associate with over twenty years of experience in the network administration and information technology training fields. He has helped hundreds of students start or improve their technology careers and earn certifications.

Table of Contents

INTRODUCTION

Why I Wrote This Book

I've spent over twenty years in the IT field, either working directly on computer systems and networks or teaching networking courses at the college level. After teaching computer networking courses for several years, I have seen that most students new to computer networking really don't have any issues with picking up the course content. They often don't have trouble passing the certification exam if they apply themselves and are determined. But almost all students tend to be deficient when it comes to troubleshooting actual networking issues. And that's what this book is about – helping you develop the troubleshooting skill needed to pass the CCENT certification exam and succeed in the field. A skill that is only built through repetition, practice and experience.

Who This Book Is For

This book is written for anyone pursuing their CCENT certification or looking to improve their troubleshooting skill as related to Cisco-based networks. Before attempting the troubleshooting exercises in this book, you'll need to have a strong familiarity with the content covered on the Cisco CCENT exam, an ability to perform basic configuration of Cisco routing and switching devices, an understanding of the common Cisco show commands, and an understanding of the OSI model and subnetting. Armed with this knowledge at the start, we'll troubleshoot a wide range of networking and connectivity issues on a variety of network topologies. The troubleshooting exercises in this book include substantial practice on standard Access Control Lists, RIP, NAT, DHCP and switch port security, among other topics you can expect to see on the ICND 100-105 CCENT exam.

What This Book Is

If you've searched for books, tutorials or video courses to help you earn your CCENT certification, or to help you become a better network technician, you may have noticed that there is no shortage of resources to help you learn the certification content. These resources are, for the most part, designed to help you *memorize* the content. But these resources don't do much to help you build the most important skill related to this knowledge – **the ability to effectively troubleshoot and diagnose connectivity problems on a real network**. That's because learning to troubleshoot, and learning to do it well, is a skill that takes a LOT of practice and repetition. Troubleshooting is one of the most important skills necessary to succeed in the IT field, one of the most difficult to obtain and master, and, in my opinion, the one major skill that separates the elite (and therefore best paid) network engineers and administrators from everyone else. This book goes beyond just memorizing show commands or troubleshooting theory – it's a collection of troubleshooting exercises that will get you thinking about the problem behind the problem and will give you a lot of repetitive practice doing so.

What This Book Is Not

Please keep in mind that this troubleshooting guide is NOT a complete study guide or an exam cram book, nor is it a replacement for the certification curriculum. **This book specifically and exclusively covers the CCENT exam objectives that are related to troubleshooting.** We will NOT be covering basic exam concepts or terminology in the book. We also will not be covering many of the exam objectives that are unrelated to troubleshooting. It is expected that you have already obtained the necessary prerequisite knowledge are now ready to build your troubleshooting ability beyond that base knowledge.

Also, just like every other technical book ever written, this book is not a substitution for hands-on experience or practice. Ideally, you've already completed a Cisco training course and are now thinking about getting certified, or you have the knowledge but don't feel fully confident in your ability to apply your skills in a live network environment. Perhaps you're already working in the field but just want to strengthen your troubleshooting ability. In any of these cases, this troubleshooting guide can help.

How This Book Is Organized

This guide provides you with troubleshooting exercises for the most important technical concepts that Cisco references in the CCENT curriculum. This book will review a group of show commands related to a major exam topic, and then provide troubleshooting exercises related to that topic. At the end of each chapter, the book will provide the solution and an explanation for each exercise.

Things to Keep in Mind

There are several things that you need to keep in mind as you work through this book:

First, please understand that some information is often purposely withheld in the exercises to create a challenge in the troubleshooting process and to force you to use the specific commands provided. In other words, you will see exercises that have topologies that do not have labels for certain interfaces or do not provide certain command outputs that would otherwise be beneficial. This is purposeful and part of the troubleshooting challenge!

Second, to help you focus on important points, some portion of the output from the show commands may be omitted.

Lastly, please keep in mind Cisco has the right to include pretty much whatever they want on their certification exams. Therefore, it is not possible to present every potential troubleshooting scenario in the book that might rear its ugly head on the exam, or on a live network. There are potentially millions of different configuration errors or combinations of errors that could be on a network, and they simply can't all be presented here. What have been included here are the most likely scenarios that I have seen based on my years of study and working with students and the Cisco curriculum. With proper study, the group of troubleshooting exercises contained in this book should be more than enough to get you where you want to go.

Network Diagrams Explained

All exercises in the book contain network diagrams that represent a sample network configuration. All diagrams will use the following graphics to represent specific network components.

Layer 3 Router, with various interfaces that may include FastEthernet, GigabitEthernet, and/or Serial interfaces, based on model. They will have a variety of configurations.

Layer 2 Switch, with various interfaces that may include FastEthernet or GigabitEthernet interfaces, based on model. They will have a variety of configurations.

Server, which may provide some network-based service, such as file sharing, email, DNS or DHCP.

Host Device/Workstation, which is attempting to connect to the network and may or may not be successful. Other devices on the network may also attempt to connect to this device, and may or may not be successful in doing so.

Straight-through Cable, used for most ethernet based connections from one device to another. Also used in examples within this book to indicate some server connections without showing additional switches or firewalls on the server subnetwork.

Crossover Cable, used for ethernet based connections between two devices that reside at the same OSI layer, such as a switch-to-switch connection or a router-to-router connection.

- - - - - -

Serial Cable, used to connect two routers that are configured with serial interfaces.

Stub Network, used to denote a network segment or subnetwork without having to document or show the switches, servers and/or host devices that reside on that network segment.

How to Complete the Exercises

Each of the exercises in this book will provide you with background information, a task, a network topology diagram, and output from one or more show commands. After reviewing the background information and task, use the command output in coordination with the network topology diagram to determine where the configuration error or errors are located, just as you would on live equipment. For example, assume an exercise provides you with the following background information and task:

> _Background Information:_ A single router corporate network has been experiencing network connectivity issues.

> _Task:_ Use the output from the troubleshooting commands to identify the two configuration errors.

From reviewing the background information, you now know that the network has a single router and connectivity has been problematic. You also know from the task that there are two errors in the command output that need to be located.

Next, review the network topology diagram. From the diagram we can determine the IP addressing of the two subnetworks and the overall configuration of the network. We also can see that some detail is purposely absent, such as interface labels and IP addressing for the two workstations.

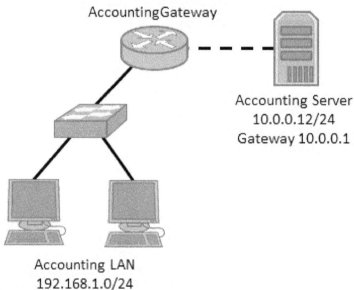

Accounting Gateway

Accounting Server
10.0.0.12/24
Gateway 10.0.0.1

Accounting LAN
192.168.1.0/24
LAN Gateway: 192.168.1.1

After reviewing the topology, continue by reviewing the command output in search of the two errors referenced in the task.

```
AccountingGateway#show running-config
Building configuration...
Current configuration : 722 bytes
!
version 15.1
no service timestamps log datetime msec
no service timestamps debug datetime msec
```

```
no service password-encryption
!
hostname AccountingGateway
!
ip cef
no ipv6 cef
!
spanning-tree mode pvst
!
interface GigabitEthernet0/0
no ip address
duplex auto
speed auto
shutdown
!
interface GigabitEthernet0/1
no ip address
duplex auto
speed auto
!
interface GigabitEthernet0/2
ip address 10.0.0.1 255.255.255.0
duplex auto
speed auto
shutdown
!
interface Vlan1
no ip address
shutdown
!
end
```

Hopefully, after careful review you located the two issues - there is no interface configured for the 192.168.1.0/24 network, and interface G0/2 is shut down. See below to see what we're specifically looking for:

AccountingGateway#show running-config
```
Building configuration...
Current configuration : 722 bytes
!
version 15.1
no service timestamps log datetime msec
no service timestamps debug datetime msec
no service password-encryption
!
hostname AccountingGateway
!
ip cef
no ipv6 cef
!
spanning-tree mode pvst
!
interface GigabitEthernet0/0
```
no ip address
```
duplex auto
speed auto
shutdown
```

```
!
interface GigabitEthernet0/1
no ip address
duplex auto
speed auto
!
interface GigabitEthernet0/2
ip address 10.0.0.1 255.255.255.0
duplex auto
speed auto
shutdown
!
interface Vlan1
no ip address
shutdown
!
end
```

If this process doesn't make much sense or you are unsure of the terminology or what the command output is telling you, you may want to go back and review the content of the certification exam some more until you feel comfortable with the concepts. If you do understand what we just reviewed here, but found it challenging, then you're in the right place, because working through the exercises in this book will greatly help you develop your troubleshooting ability. If you're ready for the challenge, then move on to chapter 1!

CHAPTER 1: Interface Configuration and Static Routing

Basic interface configuration and static routing errors are a challenge for many who are new to networking and network troubleshooting. Cisco devotes several exam topics to basic troubleshooting of both IPv4 and IPv6 interfaces, switchport errors and static routing. In this section, we'll look at the following exam objectives related to interface configuration and static routing:

> *1.8 Configure, verify, and troubleshoot IPv4 addressing and subnetting*
> *1.12 Configure, verify, and troubleshoot IPv6 addressing*
> *2.3 Troubleshoot interface and cable issues (collisions, errors, duplex, speed)*
> *3.6 Configure, verify, and troubleshoot IPv4 and IPv6 static routing*
> > *3.6.a Default route*
> > *3.6.b Network route*
> > *3.6.c Host route*
> > *3.6.d Floating static*

As you can see from the exam objectives above, you'll need to be comfortable with **configuring**, **verifying** and **troubleshooting interfaces**, **subnetting** and overall topologies that are assigned with **IPv4** and/or **IPv6** addresses. With that said, don't fall into the habit of shying away from understanding and mastering IPv6 addressing, as many people tend to do. You'll need to be comfortable with troubleshooting a configuration regardless of the addressing scheme. Switchport issues, such as duplex and speed are minor issues that you may see on the exam, but you should expect that static routing and subnetting will appear in some form. Questions that refer to an IPv4 class C /24 network subnetted down to anything from a /25 to a /30 should be expected. Other common troubleshooting problems regarding interface configuration and static routing at the CCENT level are often focused on one or more of the following issues:

1. Incorrect IPv4 or IPv6 address on a router interface.
2. Incorrect subnet mask.
3. A router interface not in an up/up state.
4. Mismatched duplex, speed, or other cable setting.
5. Static routes exiting the incorrect interface.

6. Insufficient static routes that do not accommodate for all networks that need to be reached.

The commands we primarily rely on to troubleshoot standard interface configuration and static routing issues are the *show running-config*, *show startup-config*, *show ip interface,* and *show ip route* commands, the IPv6 command *show ipv6 interface*, and *show interfaces*. The host commands *ping*, *traceroute* and *ipconfig* are also critical. Let's take a quick look at some of these troubleshooting commands now.

show running-config / show startup-config

The *show running-config* command will tell us nearly anything and everything we need to know about the switch or router configuration at the CCENT level, however you can expect that the certification exam may require you to use a command other than *show running-config* to answer a specific question to test the depth of your troubleshooting knowledge of a particular topic. Regardless, keep in mind that the *show running-config* command can tell us about interfaces, dynamic and static routes, ACLs and DHCP configurations, among many other things, and that the difference between *show running-config* and *show startup-config* is that the running config is what is running actively in RAM, and therefore is the active configuration, and the startup-config is the configuration from the last save, and what will be in play should the device reboot, assuming it is set to be loaded on bootup.

show ip interface

show ip interface is another common and highly useful command that gives us OSI layer 3 information about an interface, including any assigned ip addresses and access control lists that are specifically applied to an interface. It also has two common variants, *show ip interface brief* and *show ip interface interface-name*, which provide device-wide summary data and interface-specific detailed data, respectively.

show ipv6 interface

The IPv6 variants of the *show ip interface* commands operate in the same way as their IPv4 counterparts and provide you with the same information, but specifically for any interfaces that are running IPv6 on the device. This means you can, and should, use the *show ipv6 interface, show ipv6 interface brief*, and *show ipv6 interface interface-name* commands as needed and in the same way you use the IPv4 commands.

show interfaces

The *show interfaces* command provides us with layer 1 and layer 2 information about our interfaces, including mac addresses, hardware type, duplex, speed, and perhaps most importantly, frame or packet errors on the interface. The *show interfaces* command is your go-to when transmission on an interface is unreliable or intermittent, or you need to confirm duplex and speed settings.

ping / traceroute / tracert / ipconfig

ping and *traceroute* can be run from a host device or a networking device such as your router, so when you use these commands, consider where you're pinging or trace routing from. Let me say that again – you can ping or traceroute from a host device or from the router, which are two ways to troubleshoot connectivity from different angles.

While on a router, you can run the *ping* command without specifying the ip address, which will give you several options, including which interface on the router to ping from (to see if the router can route across itself to get to the destination) and the option to do an extended ping. The *traceroute* command shows us pinging hop by hop to our destination, which can tell us where a routing failure is occurring. *Traceroute* is Cisco specific, while the shorter *tracert* is used from a Windows command prompt. *Ipconfig* is used to view the configured ip address, default gateway and subnet mask on a Windows host machine. *Ipconfig* will also confirm that we are unable to get an address from a DHCP server. This is shown if we end up with an APIPA address, which has the first two octets of 169.254.

show ip route / show ipv6 route

show ip route and *show ipv6 route* show the routing tables as related to these two layer 3 protocols. Use these commands to see all routes that are known by the router, and how the router will route them. Additionally, the routing table will show you the route that is serving as the gateway of last resort, if there is one, and any dynamic routing protocols that are configured. An important point of clarification here: *show running-config* will show you what dynamic routing protocols you've installed but *show ip route* or *show ipv6 route* will show you how the router is routing with them. This is an important difference. Also use these commands to verify the local addressing of the router's interfaces and the connected networks they support, which are denoted with an L and C (representing Local and Connected.)

Static Route Variants

We also need to clarify the differences between the various types of static routes. Cisco wants you to be able to differentiate between default, network, host and floating static routes. Note that default static routes are simply static routes that match all packets by using 0.0.0.0/0 or IPv6's ::/0 as the destination address. Default static routes are used by the router when no other better routing option exists. Static network routes route to an entire network or subnet, whereas static host routes are defined with /32 addresses and route to a specific host. With static host routes, all bits in the subnet mask are set to 1's so the subnet mask is therefore 255.255.255.255. Lastly, floating static routes serve as backups to other routing options, and therefore are configured with a higher administrative distance than other options. To configure a static route with a higher administrative distance, add the custom administrative distance to the end of the static route command. Keep in mind that the default administrative distance of a static route is 1, which is superior to all dynamic routing protocols and inferior only to a directly connected interface.

With that said, it's time to get down to business and jump into the troubleshooting exercises. We'll start out very basic and build up more complexity from there, all while looking at a variety of common issues. Keep in mind that in many cases I've withheld some "nice-to-have" information, such as interface names or specific show commands, to force you as the troubleshooter to "reverse engineer" what you're seeing in a different way so that you build your troubleshooting skillset faster. This is critical and very practical, since in many on-the-job troubleshooting situations you won't have access to all the information you'd prefer to have. Let's get started!

EXERCISE #1 – Troubleshooting Basic Configuration Errors #1

Background Information: The Accounting department is using a single router to route between two subnetworks that contain their user LAN and their server. A network administrator has configured the router's interfaces, but the users on the Accounting LAN are reporting that they cannot connect to the accounting server, which is located on the 10.0.0.0/24 network and has the IP address of 10.0.0.12. The users on the Accounting LAN are still able to connect to each other. No other issues have been reported to the help desk.

Task: The network administrator has provided you with the following topology, but he did not document which interfaces he connected on the router. Given the topology and the show command output below, identify the two configuration errors on the router that are preventing server connectivity for the users on the Accounting LAN.

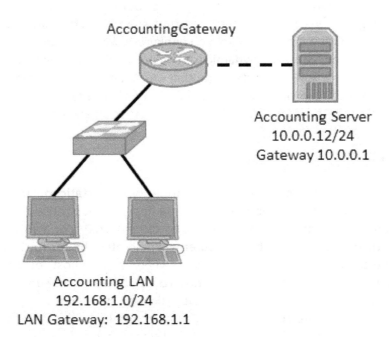

AccountingGateway

Accounting Server
10.0.0.12/24
Gateway 10.0.0.1

Accounting LAN
192.168.1.0/24
LAN Gateway: 192.168.1.1

```
AccountingGateway#show running-config
Building configuration...
Current configuration : 722 bytes
!
version 15.1
no service timestamps log datetime msec
no service timestamps debug datetime msec
no service password-encryption
!
hostname AccountingGateway
!
ip cef
no ipv6 cef
!
spanning-tree mode pvst
!
```

```
interface GigabitEthernet0/0
no ip address
duplex auto
speed auto
shutdown
!
interface GigabitEthernet0/1
ip address 192.168.1.1 255.255.255.0
duplex auto
speed auto
shutdown
!
interface GigabitEthernet0/2
ip address 10.0.0.1 255.255.255.252
duplex auto
speed auto
!
interface Vlan1
no ip address
shutdown
!
end
```

EXERCISE #2 – Troubleshooting Basic Configuration Errors #2

Background Information: A business is using a single router to route between two subnetworks that contain their user LAN and their servers. A network administrator has configured the router's interfaces, but the users are reporting that they cannot connect to the servers. No other issues have been reported to the help desk.

Task: Given the topology and the show commands output below, identify the two configuration errors on the router that are preventing server connectivity for the users on the LAN.

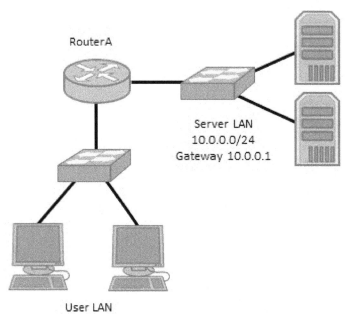

```
RouterA#show ip route
Gateway of last resort is not set

192.168.1.0/24 is variably subnetted, 2 subnets, 2 masks
C     192.168.1.0/24 is directly connected, GigabitEthernet0/1
L     192.168.1.1/32 is directly connected, GigabitEthernet0/1


RouterA#show ip interface brief
Interface            IP-Address     Status                    Protocol
GigabitEthernet0/0   unassigned     administratively down     down
GigabitEthernet0/1   192.168.1.1    up                        up
GigabitEthernet0/2   100.0.0.1      administratively down     down
Vlan1                unassigned     administratively down     down
```

EXERCISE #3 – Troubleshooting Basic Configuration Errors #3

Background Information: The Accounting department is using a single router to route between three subnetworks that contain their user LAN and their mail and file servers. The router's interfaces have been configured, but the users on the Accounting LAN are reporting that they cannot connect to the mail server, which is located on the 10.0.1.0/24 network. The users on the Accounting LAN are still able to connect to each other and can access files on their file server. No other issues have been reported.

Task: Given the topology and the show command output below, identify the configuration error on the router that is preventing mail server connectivity for the users on the Accounting LAN.

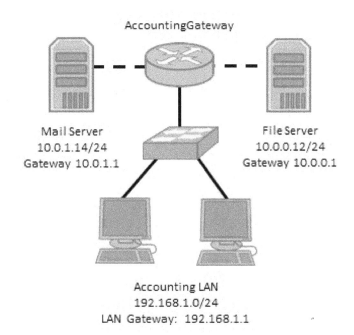

AccountingGateway

Mail Server
10.0.1.14/24
Gateway 10.0.1.1

File Server
10.0.0.12/24
Gateway 10.0.0.1

Accounting LAN
192.168.1.0/24
LAN Gateway: 192.168.1.1

```
AccountingGateway#show running-config
Building configuration...
Current configuration : 722 bytes
!
version 15.1
no service timestamps log datetime msec
no service timestamps debug datetime msec
no service password-encryption
!
hostname AccountingGateway
!
ip cef
no ipv6 cef
!
spanning-tree mode pvst
!
interface GigabitEthernet0/0
ip address 10.1.1.1 255.255.255.0
duplex auto
```

```
speed auto
!
interface GigabitEthernet0/1
ip address 192.168.1.1 255.255.255.0
duplex auto
speed auto
!
interface GigabitEthernet0/2
ip address 10.0.0.1 255.255.255.0
duplex auto
speed auto
!
interface Vlan1
no ip address
shutdown
!
end
```

EXERCISE #4 – Troubleshooting Basic Configuration Errors #4

<u>Background Information</u>: Two routers are connected via a serial connection, and each router serves a local user LAN. Users on both LANs need to have access to the file server on the 10.0.0.0/24 network. Users on the Accounting LAN can access the server, however the user on the Finance LAN cannot. No other issues have been reported.

<u>Task</u>: Use the output from the troubleshooting commands to identify the configuration error.

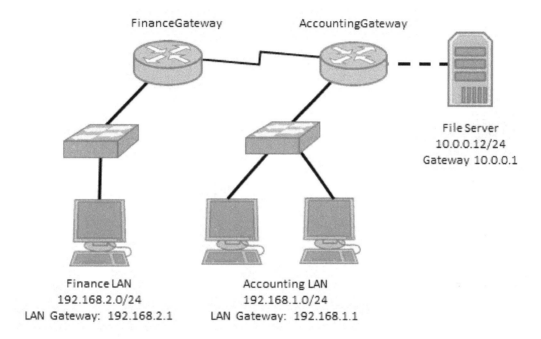

FinanceGateway   AccountingGateway

File Server
10.0.0.12/24
Gateway 10.0.0.1

Finance LAN
192.168.2.0/24
LAN Gateway: 192.168.2.1

Accounting LAN
192.168.1.0/24
LAN Gateway: 192.168.1.1

Command Prompt – 192.168.2.12

```
C:\>ping 192.168.1.1

Pinging 192.168.1.1 with 32 bytes of data:

Reply from 192.168.1.1:  bytes=32 time=2ms TTL=254
Reply from 192.168.1.1:  bytes=32 time=1ms TTL=254
Reply from 192.168.1.1:  bytes=32 time=4ms TTL=254
Reply from 192.168.1.1:  bytes=32 time=4ms TTL=254

C:\>ping 10.0.0.1

Pinging 10.0.0.1 with 32 bytes of data:

Reply from 192.168.2.1:  Destination host unreachable.
Reply from 192.168.2.1:  Destination host unreachable.
Reply from 192.168.2.1:  Destination host unreachable.
Reply from 192.168.2.1:  Destination host unreachable.
```

```
FinanceGateway#show running-config
Building configuration...
Current configuration : 908 bytes
!
version 15.1
no service timestamps log datetime msec
!
hostname FinanceGateway
!
interface GigabitEthernet0/0
no ip address
duplex auto
speed auto
shutdown
!
interface GigabitEthernet0/1
ip address 192.168.2.1 255.255.255.0
duplex auto
speed auto
!
interface GigabitEthernet0/2
no ip address
duplex auto
speed auto
shutdown
!
interface Serial0/0/0
ip address 10.1.1.5 255.255.255.252
clock rate 64000
!
interface Serial0/0/1
no ip address
clock rate 2000000
shutdown
!
interface Vlan1
no ip address
shutdown
!
ip classless
ip route 192.168.1.0 255.255.255.0 Serial0/0/0
!
line con 0
!
line aux 0
!
line vty 0 4
login
!
end
```

```
AccountingGateway#show running-config
Building configuration...
Current configuration : 903 bytes
!
version 15.1
no service timestamps log datetime msec
!
hostname AccountingGateway
!
interface GigabitEthernet0/0
no ip address
duplex auto
speed auto
shutdown
!
interface GigabitEthernet0/1
ip address 192.168.1.1 255.255.255.0
duplex auto
speed auto
!
interface GigabitEthernet0/2
ip address 10.0.0.1 255.255.255.0
duplex auto
speed auto
!
interface Serial0/0/0
ip address 10.1.1.6 255.255.255.252
!
interface Serial0/0/1
no ip address
clock rate 2000000
shutdown
!
interface Vlan1
no ip address
shutdown
!
ip classless
ip route 192.168.2.0 255.255.255.0 Serial0/0/0
!
line con 0
!
line aux 0
!
line vty 0 4
login
!
end
```

EXERCISE #5 – Troubleshooting Basic Configuration Errors #5

Background Information: A three-router, corporate metropolitan area network has been experiencing network connectivity issues. At this point, you haven't been provided with more information regarding where the connectivity issues are occurring. All location networks use the first available IP address as their gateway.

Task: Use the output from the troubleshooting commands to identify the two configuration errors.

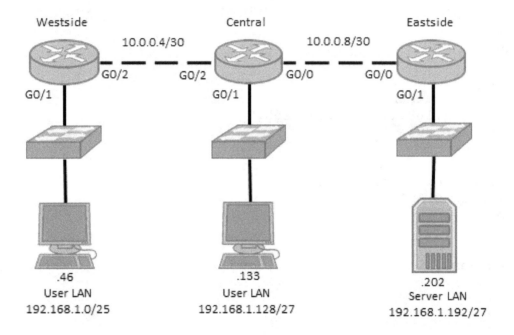

Westside	Central	Eastside

10.0.0.4/30   10.0.0.8/30

GO/2   GO/2   GO/0   GO/0

GO/1   GO/1   GO/1

.46   .133   .202
User LAN   User LAN   Server LAN
192.168.1.0/25   192.168.1.128/27   192.168.1.192/27

Command Prompt – 192.168.1.202

```
C:\>tracert 10.0.0.5

Tracing route to 10.0.0.5 over a maximum of 30 hops:

1 0 ms  0 ms    0 ms    192.168.1.193
2 10 ms         3 ms    10 ms   10.0.0.9
3 *      *      *       Request timed out.
4 *      *      *       Request timed out.
5 *      *      *       Request timed out.
```

```
Eastside#show ip route

Gateway of last resort is 10.0.0.9 to network 0.0.0.0

      10.0.0.0/8 is variably subnetted, 2 subnets, 2 masks
C         10.0.0.8/30 is directly connected, GigabitEthernet0/0
L         10.0.0.10/32 is directly connected, GigabitEthernet0/0
      192.168.1.0/24 is variably subnetted, 2 subnets, 2 masks
C         192.168.1.192/27 is directly connected, GigabitEthernet0/1
```

```
L           192.168.1.193/32 is directly connected, GigabitEthernet0/1
S*          0.0.0.0/0 [1/0] via 10.0.0.9
```

Central#show ip route

```
Gateway of last resort is not set

        10.0.0.0/8 is variably subnetted, 4 subnets, 2 masks
C           10.0.0.4/30 is directly connected, GigabitEthernet0/2
L           10.0.0.6/32 is directly connected, GigabitEthernet0/2
C           10.0.0.8/30 is directly connected, GigabitEthernet0/0
L           10.0.0.9/32 is directly connected, GigabitEthernet0/0
        192.168.1.0/24 is variably subnetted, 4 subnets, 3 masks
S           192.168.1.0/25 is directly connected, GigabitEthernet0/2
C           192.168.1.128/27 is directly connected, GigabitEthernet0/1
L           192.168.1.129/32 is directly connected, GigabitEthernet0/1
S           192.168.1.192/28 is directly connected, GigabitEthernet0/0
```

Westside#show ip route

```
Gateway of last resort is 0.0.0.0 to network 0.0.0.0

        10.0.0.0/8 is variably subnetted, 2 subnets, 2 masks
C           10.0.0.4/30 is directly connected, GigabitEthernet0/2
L           10.0.0.5/32 is directly connected, GigabitEthernet0/2
        192.168.1.0/24 is variably subnetted, 2 subnets, 2 masks
C           192.168.1.0/25 is directly connected, GigabitEthernet0/1
L           192.168.1.1/32 is directly connected, GigabitEthernet0/1
S*      0.0.0.0/0 is directly connected, GigabitEthernet0/1
```

EXERCISE #6 – Troubleshooting Basic Configuration Errors #6

Background Information: Users in Building 2 have contacted the help desk to report that they are unable to connect to the File Server. You have verified that the File Server is accessible to users in Building 3.

Task: Use the output from the troubleshooting commands to identify the configuration error.

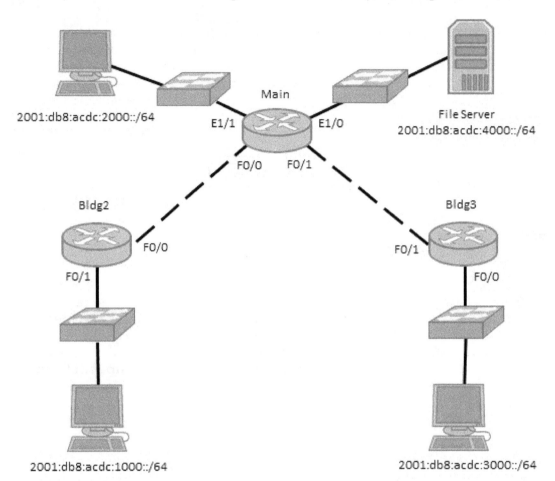

2001:db8:acdc:2000::/64

Main

E1/1   E1/0

File Server
2001:db8:acdc:4000::/64

F0/0   F0/1

Bldg2

F0/0

F0/1

Bldg3

F0/1

F0/0

2001:db8:acdc:1000::/64

2001:db8:acdc:3000::/64

```
Main#show ipv6 interface brief
FastEthernet0/0          [down/down]
     2001:DB8:ACDC:5000::2
FastEthernet0/1          [up/up]
     2001:DB8:ACDC:6000::1
Ethernet1/0              [up/up]
     2001:DB8:ACDC:4000::1
Ethernet1/1              [up/up]
     2001:DB8:ACDC:2000::1
Ethernet1/2              [administratively down/down]
Ethernet1/3              [administratively down/down]
```

```
Bldg2#show ipv6 interface brief
FastEthernet0/0        [down/down]
     2001:DB8:ACDC:1000::1
FastEthernet0/1        [up/up]
     2001:DB8:ACDC:5000::1
Vlan1 [administratively down/down]
```

EXERCISE #7 – Troubleshooting Basic Configuration Errors #7

Background Information: A co-worker is planning to implement a three-router network that will be routed statically. She has entered the planned static routes in her test network, but she is unable to achieve full network connectivity.

Task: Use the command output below to identify the two static route configuration errors.

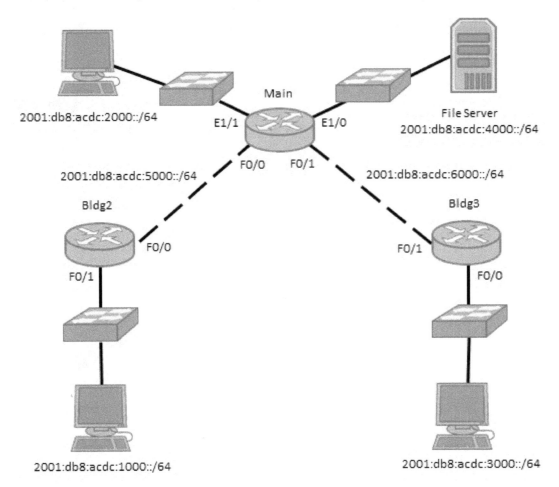

```
Bldg2#show running-config | include route
ipv6 route 2001:DB8:ACDC:2000::/64 FastEthernet0/0
2001:DB8:ACDC:5000::2
ipv6 route 2001:DB8:ACDC:3000::/64 FastEthernet0/0
2001:DB8:ACDC:5000::2
ipv6 route 2001:DB8:ACDC:4000::/64 FastEthernet0/0
2001:DB8:ACDC:5000::2
ipv6 route 2001:DB8:ACDC:6000::/64 FastEthernet0/0
2001:DB8:ACDC:5000::2
```

```
Main#show running-config | include route
ipv6 route 2001:DB8:ACDC:1000::/52 FastEthernet0/0
2001:DB8:ACDC:5000::1
ipv6 route 2001:DB8:ACDC:3000::/52 FastEthernet0/0
2001:DB8:ACDC:6000::2


Bldg3#show running-config | include route
ipv6 route ::/0 FastEthernet0/1 2001:DB8:ACAC:6000::1
```

SOLUTIONS TO EXERCISES FOR CHAPTER 1

SOLUTION – EXERCISE #1

We have a limited amount of information to work from in this exercise; however, we can verify that we are viewing the running configuration for the AccountingGateway router based on the command issued and the hostname entry in the output. Even though the topology doesn't define the specific interfaces on the router that are being used to serve the two LANs, we can determine, based on the *show running-config* output, that they are interfaces G0/1 and G0/2 (specifically, interface G0/1 is the gateway for the Accounting LAN with the IP address of 192.168.1.1, and interface G0/2 is serving the server network with a gateway IP address of 10.0.0.1). Based on the configuration output, interface G0/1 apparently has not been issued the *no shutdown* command to have been moved into an up state, and interface G0/2 has a subnet mask of 255.255.255.252, which is a /30 network, yet the topology specifically documents that the server LAN is a /24 network. The *show ip interface* command could also verify the interface issues shown here.

SOLUTION – EXERCISE #2

Just as in exercise #1, we have a limited amount of information to work from. With the *show ip route* command provided, we see that the routing table is only registering one known network, which is the 192.168.1.0/24 user network. The 10.0.0.0/24 server network should appear in the routing table because it is directly connected, but it does not. A possibility is that the interface serving the server LAN is down for some reason, which is confirmed in the *show ip interface brief* output. Here we see that interface G0/2 is administratively down, meaning the administrator must input the *no shutdown* command to bring the interface up. Even if the administrator brings the interface up, issues will still occur, as we can also see that the interface is incorrectly addressed with the 100.0.0.1 IP address, instead of the correct 10.0.0.1 address.

SOLUTION – EXERCISE #3

With the show command provided, we can verify that we're viewing the running configuration for the AccountingGateway router based on the command name and the hostname entry in the output. The topology doesn't define the specific interfaces on the router that are being used to serve the LANs, but by looking closely, we can see that interface G0/0 is serving the nonexistent 10.1.1.0/24 network. The correct IP address should be 10.0.1.1 as documented in the topology. Interfaces G0/1 and G0/2 are correctly configured.

SOLUTION - EXERCISE #4

In this two router exercise, the router interfaces are configured correctly, but the FinanceGateway router has no static route to the 10.0.0.0/24 network, and therefore has no way to get to the File Server. A tip-off is that the ping command was successful to connect to the 192.168.1.0/24 network gateway, but not to the 10.0.0.0/24 gateway. This tells us that our Finance LAN user can transmit out of her network to the AccountingGateway router and into the Accounting LAN, and back, but just doesn't have a means to get to the file server LAN. In a topology such as this where there are no dynamic routing protocols present and we are relying on static routing, each router should have a static route to all non-directly connected networks that we need to access, or a gateway of last resort. Note that there is no gateway of last resort command in the *show running-config* output either.

SOLUTION - EXERCISE #5

This is the first exercise where substantial IPv4 subnetting comes into play. In this exercise, we have two configuration errors, one of which is difficult to locate. First, note from the Westside router's *show ip route* command output that the Westside router's default static route is sending all traffic out of interface G0/1, which is an interface that is being used for the local LAN. Instead, this route should have an exit interface of G0/2, which is the exit interface used to get to all other networks. As written, the Westside router will send all traffic destined for anywhere else on the network directly back into its own LAN. The traceroute times out at the Westside router because it attempts to send an ICMP message to 192.168.1.202 out of its G0/1 interface rather than G0/2. For the second error, the Central router is able to route to the 192.168.1.192 network, however it is configured as a /28 instead of the correct /27. This is not a critical failure in this situation for the server at 192.168.1.202 because its IP address still falls within the range of that network as well, but it will cause routing issues for other IP addresses that do not fall within that range and therefore should be corrected.

SOLUTION - EXERCISE #6

In this IPv6 exercise, the Bldg2 router has the IPv6 addresses on its two interfaces assigned to the opposite, and therefore incorrect interfaces. Interface F0/0 is assigned the 2001:db8:acdc:1000::1/64 IPv6 address, when this address should be assigned to interface F0/1. Likewise, interface F0/1 is assigned the 2001:db8:acdc:5000::1/64 address, which should be assigned to interface F0/0. Because of this reversal, the link between the Bldg2 and Main routers is down. Correcting the IPv6 addressing on the Bldg2 router and bringing the link back up would solve the issue.

SOLUTION – EXERCISE #7

In this exercise, we are viewing the static routing section of the running configuration for each router in the network. There are two errors within the static routes. First, the Main router is sending traffic destined for the 2001:db8:acdc:3000::/52 network out interface F0/0, instead of F0/1. The difference of the routing prefix (/64 as documented and /52 as shown in the command output) is not an issue, as a subnetted /52 IPv6 address in this case still indicates a 3000 subnet ID. The issue is with the exit interface only. Additionally, there is an error in Bldg3's default static route next hop address. It is written as ACAC instead of ACDC. While the difference is slight, it is still enough to cause a failure.

CHAPTER 2: Dynamic Routing With RIP

Ah, RIP. The interior gateway routing protocol that no one cares about, and even fewer network administrators use. All joking aside, for some reason Cisco has added RIP (the Routing Information Protocol) to the CCENT exam objectives and removed the more prevalent OSPF and EIGRP protocols from the exam. Fortunately, you only need to concern yourself with the IPv4 Implementation of RIP, specifically RIPv2.

While RIP has many drawbacks in large-scale enterprise implementations, Cisco does have a point in that it is a decent protocol to use to introduce beginning network technicians to the concepts and challenges of dynamic routing, and RIP does perform decently well on small networks. Its metric is also easy to calculate, since it's measured by hop count, and with RIP we don't have to concern ourselves with more complex features of the other protocols, such as OSPF's multiple areas and EIGRP's k values.

In this section, we'll look at the following exam objective related to dynamic routing and the RIP dynamic routing protocol:

> *3.7 Configure, verify, and troubleshoot RIPv2 for IPv4 (excluding authentication, filtering, manual summarization, redistribution)*

Common errors related to RIP include:

1. Using RIP version 1 instead of version 2.
2. Using mismatched versions of RIP on different routers in the topology, which will cause failure.
3. Incorrectly identifying passive interfaces.
4. Misconfiguring the auto-summary command.

There are a few show commands that can assist us in determining where RIP is configured incorrectly. These commands are the usual standbys *show running-config* and *show ip route* from chapter 1, as well as the *show ip protocols* command. Let's look at this new command now.

show ip protocols

The *show ip protocols* command displays specific settings for any layer 3 IPv4 routing protocols that are configured on the router, including information about routing protocol versions, timers, router ID's and auto-summary settings. Use this command as a secondary method to the *show running-config* for determining which layer 3 protocols are installed and operational on the router. This command will also provide protocol information for OSPF and EIGRP.

show ip rip database

The *show ip rip database* command confirms the networks that are in RIP's database on that router, and how those networks were learned. This is similar in usage at the CCENT level to the *show ip route* command, which displays the full routing table.

EXERCISE #8 – Troubleshooting Routing Information Protocol #1

Background Information: All users on the Westside and Central User LANs require access to the Server LAN, but users on the Westside LAN are reporting that they do not have connectivity to the Server LAN. Users on the Central LAN are still able to connect to the Server LAN.

Task: Use the output from the troubleshooting commands to identify the configuration error.

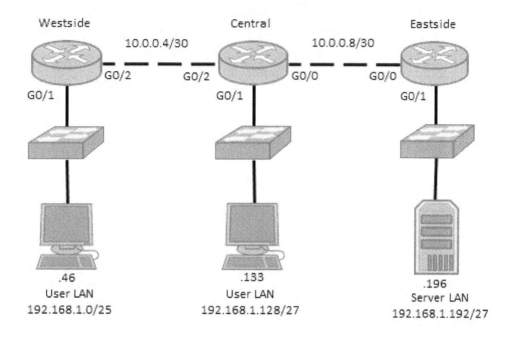

```
Command Prompt – 192.168.1.133

C:\>ping 192.168.1.46

Pinging 192.168.1.46 with 32 bytes of data:

Request timed out.
Request timed out.
Request timed out.
Request timed out.
```

```
Central#show ip route

Gateway of last resort is not set

      10.0.0.0/8 is variably subnetted, 4 subnets, 2 masks
C        10.0.0.4/30 is directly connected, GigabitEthernet0/2
L        10.0.0.6/32 is directly connected, GigabitEthernet0/2
C        10.0.0.8/30 is directly connected, GigabitEthernet0/0
L        10.0.0.9/32 is directly connected, GigabitEthernet0/0
      192.168.1.0/24 is variably subnetted, 3 subnets, 2 masks
C        192.168.1.128/27 is directly connected, GigabitEthernet0/1
```

```
L      192.168.1.129/32 is directly connected, GigabitEthernet0/1
R      192.168.1.192/27 [120/1] via 10.0.0.10, 00:00:14,
GigabitEthernet0/0
```

Westside#show running-config
```
Building configuration...

Current configuration : 814 bytes
!
version 15.1
no service timestamps log datetime msec
no service timestamps debug datetime msec
no service password-encryption
!
hostname Westside
!
ip cef
no ipv6 cef
!
interface GigabitEthernet0/0
no ip address
duplex auto
speed auto
shutdown
!
interface GigabitEthernet0/1
ip address 192.168.1.1 255.255.255.128
duplex auto
speed auto
!
interface GigabitEthernet0/2
ip address 10.0.0.5 255.255.255.252
duplex auto
speed auto
!
interface Vlan1
no ip address
shutdown
!
router rip
version 2
passive-interface GigabitEthernet0/1
network 10.0.0.0
no auto-summary
!
ip classless
!
ip flow-export version 9
!
end
```

EXERCISE #9 – Troubleshooting Routing Information Protocol #2

Background Information: Users on the Westside and Central User LANs are experiencing connectivity issues with each other. You notice that users on the Central User LAN are still able to access the Server LAN, however users on the Westside User LAN are not.

Task: Use the output from the troubleshooting commands to identify the configuration error.

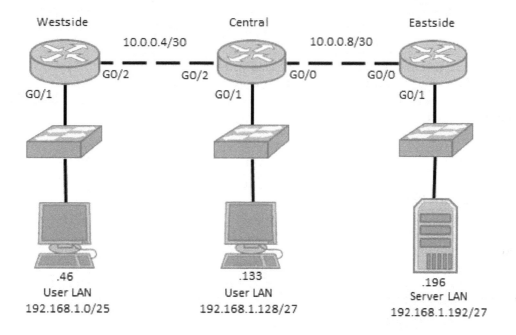

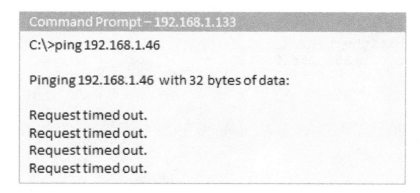

```
Command Prompt – 192.168.1.133

C:\>ping 192.168.1.46

Pinging 192.168.1.46 with 32 bytes of data:

Request timed out.
Request timed out.
Request timed out.
Request timed out.
```

Central#show ip route

```
Gateway of last resort is not set

   10.0.0.0/8 is variably subnetted, 4 subnets, 2 masks
C    10.0.0.4/30 is directly connected, GigabitEthernet0/2
L    10.0.0.6/32 is directly connected, GigabitEthernet0/2
C    10.0.0.8/30 is directly connected, GigabitEthernet0/0
L    10.0.0.9/32 is directly connected, GigabitEthernet0/0
   192.168.1.0/24 is variably subnetted, 3 subnets, 2 masks
C    192.168.1.128/27 is directly connected, GigabitEthernet0/1
```

```
L    192.168.1.129/32 is directly connected, GigabitEthernet0/1
R    192.168.1.192/27    [120/1]    via    10.0.0.10,    00:00:16,
GigabitEthernet0/0
```

Westside#show running-config
```
Building configuration...

Current configuration : 824 bytes
!
version 15.1
no service timestamps log datetime msec
no service timestamps debug datetime msec
no service password-encryption
!
hostname Westside
!
ip cef
no ipv6 cef
!
interface GigabitEthernet0/0
no ip address
duplex auto
speed auto
shutdown
!
interface GigabitEthernet0/1
ip address 192.168.1.1 255.255.255.128
duplex auto
speed auto
!
interface GigabitEthernet0/2
ip address 10.0.0.5 255.255.255.252
duplex auto
speed auto
!
interface Vlan1
no ip address
shutdown
!
router rip
passive-interface GigabitEthernet0/1
network 10.0.0.0
network 192.168.1.0
no auto-summary
!
ip classless
!
ip flow-export version 9
!
line con 0
!
line aux 0
```

```
!
line vty 0 4
login
!
end
```

Central#show running-config
```
Building configuration...

Current configuration : 848 bytes
!
version 15.1
no service timestamps log datetime msec
no service timestamps debug datetime msec
no service password-encryption
!
hostname Central
!
ip cef
no ipv6 cef
!
spanning-tree mode pvst
!
interface GigabitEthernet0/0
ip address 10.0.0.9 255.255.255.252
duplex auto
speed auto
!
interface GigabitEthernet0/1
ip address 192.168.1.129 255.255.255.224
duplex auto
speed auto
!
interface GigabitEthernet0/2
ip address 10.0.0.6 255.255.255.252
duplex auto
speed auto
!
interface Vlan1
no ip address
shutdown
!
router rip
version 2
passive-interface GigabitEthernet0/1
network 10.0.0.0
network 192.168.1.0
no auto-summary
!
ip classless
!
ip flow-export version 9
```

```
!
line con 0
!
line aux 0
!
line vty 0 4
login
!
end
```

EXERCISE #10 – Troubleshooting Routing Information Protocol #3

Background Information: Users on the Finance and Accounting LANs are reporting that they cannot connect with each other. They were able to connect earlier in the day.

Task: Use the output from the troubleshooting commands to identify the configuration error.

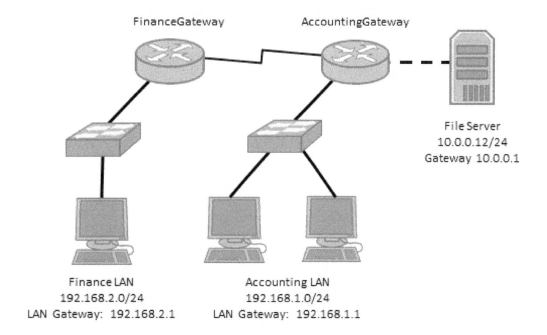

```
FinanceGateway#show ip route
Gateway of last resort is not set

10.0.0.0/8 is variably subnetted, 3 subnets, 3 masks
R    10.0.0.0/24 is possibly down, routing via 10.1.1.6, Serial0/0/0
C    10.1.1.4/30 is directly connected, Serial0/0/0
L    10.1.1.5/32 is directly connected, Serial0/0/0
R    192.168.1.0/24 is possibly down, routing via 10.1.1.6, Serial0/0/0
192.168.2.0/24 is variably subnetted, 2 subnets, 2 masks
C    192.168.2.0/24 is directly connected, GigabitEthernet0/1
L    192.168.2.1/32 is directly connected, GigabitEthernet0/1


AccountingGateway#show ip protocols
Routing Protocol is "rip"
Sending updates every 30 seconds, next due in 23 seconds
Invalid after 180 seconds, hold down 180, flushed after 240
Outgoing update filter list for all interfaces is not set
Incoming update filter list for all interfaces is not set
Redistributing: rip
Automatic network summarization is not in effect
Maximum path: 4
Routing for Networks:
     10.0.0.0
```

```
      192.168.1.0
Passive Interface(s):
      Serial0/0/0
Routing Information Sources:
      Gateway     Distance   Last Update
      10.1.1.5    120        00:00:13
Distance: (default is 120)
```

EXERCISE #11 – Troubleshooting Routing Information Protocol #4

Background Information: Users on the User LANs in Building 1 and Building 2 are not able to connect to each other. A network technician has confirmed that the host devices are correctly configured, as are the interfaces on the router. You suspect that a misconfiguration in RIP may be the issue.

Task: Use the output from the troubleshooting commands to identify the configuration error.

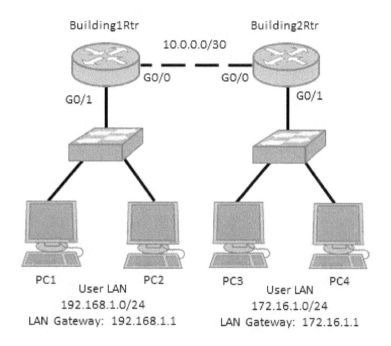

```
Building1Rtr#show ip rip database
10.0.0.0/30          auto-summary
10.0.0.0/30          directly connected, GigabitEthernet0/0
192.168.1.0/24       auto-summary
192.168.1.0/24       directly connected, GigabitEthernet0/1


Building2Rtr#show ip rip database
10.0.0.0/30          auto-summary
10.0.0.0/30          directly connected, GigabitEthernet0/0
172.16.1.0/24        auto-summary
172.16.1.0/24        directly connected, GigabitEthernet0/1
192.168.1.0/24       auto-summary
192.168.1.0/24
      [1] via 10.0.0.1, 00:00:18, GigabitEthernet0/0


Building2Rtr#show running-config
Building configuration...

Current configuration : 1038 bytes
!
```

```
version 15.1
no service timestamps log datetime msec
no service timestamps debug datetime msec
no service password-encryption
!
hostname Building2Rtr
!
interface GigabitEthernet0/0
ip address 10.0.0.2 255.255.255.252
duplex auto
speed auto
!
interface GigabitEthernet0/1
ip address 172.16.1.1 255.255.255.0
duplex auto
speed auto
!
interface GigabitEthernet0/2
no ip address
duplex auto
speed auto
shutdown
!
interface Vlan1
no ip address
shutdown
!
router rip
version 2
network 10.0.0.0
no auto-summary
!
end
```

SOLUTIONS TO EXERCISES FOR CHAPTER 2

SOLUTION – EXERCISE #8

In this exercise, the Westside router is advertising its point-to-point network (10.0.0.4/30), but it is not advertising the user LAN that it supports (192.168.1.0/25). We know this because the *network 192.168.1.0* line is missing from the *show running-config* output in the RIP section on the Westside router. If the Westside router fails to advertise its network, as it is doing in this example, no other router will be able to learn about the network, and it will therefore be unrouteable. This is causing the *show ip route* command output from the Central router to not display a route to the 192.168.1.0/25 network.

SOLUTION – EXERCISE #9

In this exercise, the Central router is running version 2 of RIP, as noted in the *show running-config* command output under the RIP section. However, the Westside router is not running version 2. We can confirm that simply because the "version 2" line in the *show running-config* output is missing on the Westside router. This version mismatch of RIP between two neighboring routers is enough to disrupt convergence and routing, because a router enabled with RIP version 2 cannot receive and process RIP version 1 updates.

SOLUTION – EXERCISE #10

By reviewing the *show ip route* command output from the FinanceGateway router, we can see that RIP is in the routing table, but all networks learned through RIP are reporting as "possibly down". This is due to the FinanceGateway router no longer receiving expected updates from RIP. From the *show ip protocols* command output on the AccountingGateway router, we see the culprit of our issue – the Serial0/0/0 interface is now listed as passive; however, it should not be passive, as it needs to send out routing updates. With dynamic routing protocols, any interface listed as passive will not have protocol updates sent out, which in this case is stopping RIP communication between the two routers. The fact that the networks were learned via RIP and were in the routing table of the FinanceGateway router but are transitioning to the state of "possibly down" indicates that a change was made and routing was functional in the recent past.

SOLUTION – EXERCISE #11

This exercise contains two user LANs and a point-to-point network and provides us with *show ip rip database* command output from both routers. With this information, we can see that the Building1Rtr router does not have the 172.16.1.0 network in its RIP database, while the Building2Rtr does have the 192.168.1.0 network in its RIP database. Further investigation into the *show running-config* confirms that the RIP configuration on the Building2Rtr is not set to advertise the 172.16.1.0/24 network. In this exercise, RIP is functioning correctly between the two routers, but the Building2Rtr is not letting the Building1Rtr know about its 172.16.1.0/24 network.

CHAPTER 3: Standard Access Control Lists

A lot of people have trouble getting the hang of access control lists. ACLs are certainly a topic that you'll want to spend time on and get down pat when preparing for the CCENT certification exam. Fortunately, Cisco has modified the ICND1/CCENT 100-105 exam objectives regarding ACLs, and specifically stated that only *standard* ACLs are now covered, as compared to the prior version of the exam, which covered both standard and the more complex *extended* ACLs.

ACLs are mentioned in ICND1/CCENT 100-105 exam objective 4.6:

> *4.6 Configure, verify, and troubleshoot IPv4 standard numbered and named access list for routed interfaces*

Note from the exam objective above that you'll need to be able to **configure**, **verify** and **troubleshoot** both **numbered** and **named standard** ACLs, but only for **IPv4**. You should expect to see at least one question on the exam specifically regarding verification and troubleshooting of ACLs. Common troubleshooting questions regarding ACLs at the CCENT level are often focused on one or more of the following issues:

1. Traffic in the ACL is denied before it is permitted, thus rendering it denied.
2. An ACL is placed on the proper interface, but in the wrong direction.
3. An ACL is placed on the wrong interface, or even the wrong router.
4. An ACL is specifying source traffic from the wrong IP address or subnet.
5. An ACL is written correctly but is not applied to an interface at all.
6. An ACL is placed on an interface that the target traffic does not flow through.

The show commands used to troubleshoot standard ACLs are:

show access-lists

The *show access-lists* command shows all access lists installed on a router, regardless of protocol. This command does not verify on which interface or interfaces or in which direction the access lists are placed, so keep in mind that just because an ACL exists and is shown in the *show access-lists* output doesn't mean that it's set up to do anything. The second step of ACL placement on an interface is required as well.

show ip interface

The *show ip interface* command is used to verify which interface or interfaces have an ACL applied to them and whether they are inbound or outbound. The *show running-config* command will verify this information as well.

Wild Card Masks

Please also keep in mind that ACLs do use wild card masks, which are the inverse of a subnet mask (such as a wild card mask of 0.0.0.255 to identify a /24 network with a subnet mask of 255.255.255.0). ACL commands that specify a specific host are indicated with a wild card of 0.0.0.0.

EXERCISE #12 – Troubleshooting a Standard Access Control List #1

Background Information: Two routers serving two different buildings on a corporate campus are connected via an Ethernet connection. A network administrator writes a standard ACL on the Building2Rtr router to block traffic from the user at 192.168.100.11 to the file server at 10.0.1.15, while still permitting all other users from that network, but the user is still able to access the file server. No other networking issues have been reported to the helpdesk.

Task: Use the output from the troubleshooting commands provided to identify the configuration error.

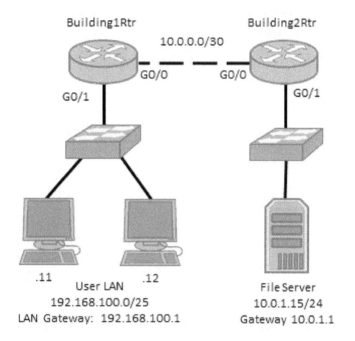

```
Building2Rtr#show access-lists
Standard IP access list BlockDot11
    10 permit 192.168.100.0 0.0.0.127
    20 deny host 192.168.100.11
```

```
Building2Rtr#show ip interface g0/0
GigabitEthernet0/0 is up, line protocol is up (connected)
    Internet address is 10.0.0.2/30
    Broadcast address is 255.255.255.255
    Address determined by setup command
    MTU is 1500 bytes
    Helper address is not set
    Directed broadcast forwarding is disabled
    Outgoing access list is not set
    Inbound access list is not set
    Proxy ARP is enabled
    Security level is default
    Split horizon is enabled
```

Building2Rtr#show ip interface g0/1
```
GigabitEthernet0/1 is up, line protocol is up (connected)
   Internet address is 10.0.1.1/24
   Broadcast address is 255.255.255.255
   Address determined by setup command
   MTU is 1500 bytes
   Helper address is not set
   Directed broadcast forwarding is disabled
   Outgoing access list is BlockDot11
   Inbound access list is not set
   Proxy ARP is enabled
   Security level is default
   Split horizon is enabled
```

Building2Rtr#show ip interface g0/1
```
GigabitEthernet0/1 is up, line protocol is up (connected)
   Internet address is 10.0.1.1/24
```

EXERCISE #13 – Troubleshooting a Standard Access Control List #2

Background Information: An organization is implementing a three-router WAN configuration with multiple user LANs. A network administrator writes a standard ACL on the New York router to block traffic from the user at 192.168.1.11 to the file server at 10.0.1.82, while still permitting all other users from that network. He notices that the user is still able to access the file server. No other networking issues have been reported to the helpdesk.

Task: Use the output from the troubleshooting commands provided to identify the configuration error.

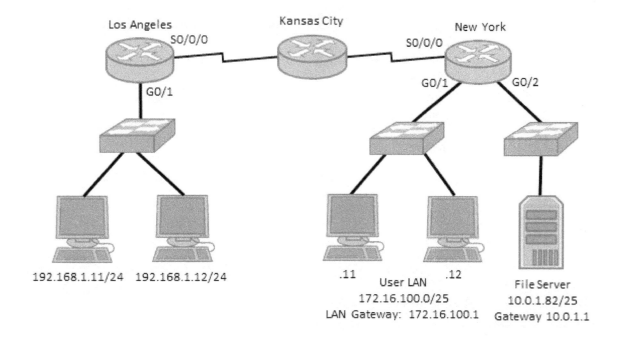

```
NewYork#show access-lists
Standard IP access list BlockDot11
    10 deny host 192.168.1.11
    20 permit any


NewYork#show running-config
Building configuration...

Current configuration : 1050 bytes
!
version 15.1
no service timestamps log datetime msec
no service timestamps debug datetime msec
no service password-encryption
!
hostname NewYork
!
interface GigabitEthernet0/0
no ip address
```

```
duplex auto
speed auto
shutdown
!
interface GigabitEthernet0/1
ip address 172.16.100.1 255.255.255.128
ip access-group BlockDot11 out
duplex auto
speed auto
!
interface GigabitEthernet0/2
ip address 10.0.1.1 255.255.255.128
duplex auto
speed auto
!
interface Serial0/0/0
ip address 10.0.0.6 255.255.255.252
clock rate 64000
!
interface Serial0/0/1
no ip address
clock rate 2000000
shutdown
!
interface Vlan1
no ip address
shutdown
!
router rip
version 2
network 10.0.0.0
network 172.16.0.0
no auto-summary
!
ip access-list standard BlockDot11
deny host 192.168.1.11
permit any
!
End
```

EXERCISE #14 – Troubleshooting a Standard Access Control List #3

Background Information: An organization is implementing a three-router WAN configuration with multiple user LANs. A network administrator writes a standard ACL on the New York router to block traffic from the user at 192.168.1.11 to the file server at 10.0.1.82, while still permitting all other users from that network, however the user is still able to access the file server. No other networking issues have been reported to the helpdesk.

Task: Use the output from the troubleshooting commands provided to identify the configuration error.

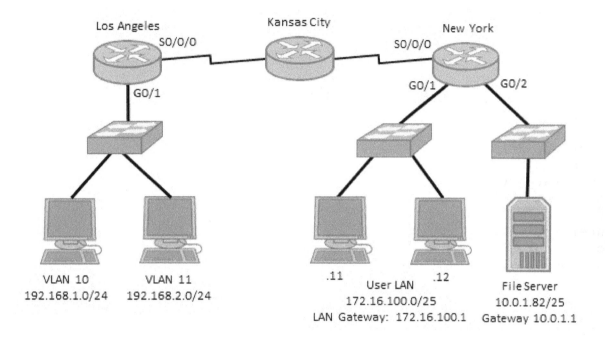

```
NewYork#show access-lists
Standard IP access list BlockDot11
    10 deny host 192.168.11.11
    20 permit any


NewYork#show running-config
Building configuration...

Current configuration : 1050 bytes
!
version 15.1
no service timestamps log datetime msec
no service timestamps debug datetime msec
no service password-encryption
!
hostname NewYork
!
interface GigabitEthernet0/0
no ip address
```

```
duplex auto
speed auto
shutdown
!
interface GigabitEthernet0/1
ip address 172.16.100.1 255.255.255.128
duplex auto
speed auto
!
interface GigabitEthernet0/2
ip address 10.0.1.1 255.255.255.128
ip access-group BlockDot11 out
duplex auto
speed auto
!
interface Serial0/0/0
ip address 10.0.0.6 255.255.255.252
clock rate 64000
!
interface Serial0/0/1
no ip address
clock rate 2000000
shutdown
!
interface Vlan1
no ip address
shutdown
!
router rip
version 2
network 10.0.0.0
network 172.16.0.0
no auto-summary
!
ip access-list standard BlockDot11
deny host 192.168.11.11
permit any
!
end
```

EXERCISE #15 – Troubleshooting a Standard Access Control List #4

Background Information: An organization is implementing a two-router WAN configuration with multiple user LANs. A network administrator writes a standard ACL on the New York router to block traffic from the user at 172.16.100.12 to the file server at 10.0.1.82, while still permitting all other users from that network, but the user is still able to access the file server. No other networking issues have been reported to the helpdesk.

Task: Use the output from the troubleshooting commands provided to identify the configuration error.

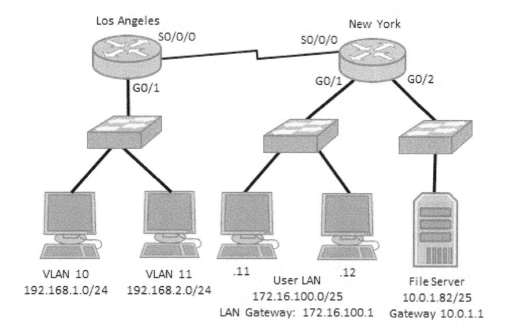

```
NewYork#show access-lists
Standard IP access list BlockDot12
    10 deny host 172.16.100.12
    20 permit any


NewYork#show running-config
Building configuration...

Current configuration : 1050 bytes
!
version 15.1
no service timestamps log datetime msec
no service timestamps debug datetime msec
no service password-encryption
!
hostname NewYork
!
interface GigabitEthernet0/0
no ip address
```

```
duplex auto
speed auto
shutdown
!
interface GigabitEthernet0/1
ip address 172.16.100.1 255.255.255.128
duplex auto
speed auto
!
interface GigabitEthernet0/2
ip address 10.0.1.1 255.255.255.128
ip access-group BlockDot12 in
duplex auto
speed auto
!
interface Serial0/0/0
ip address 10.0.0.6 255.255.255.252
clock rate 64000
!
interface Serial0/0/1
no ip address
clock rate 2000000
shutdown
!
interface Vlan1
no ip address
shutdown
!
router rip
version 2
network 10.0.0.0
network 172.16.0.0
no auto-summary
!
ip access-list standard BlockDot12
deny host 172.16.100.12
permit any
!
end
```

EXERCISE #16 – Troubleshooting a Standard Access Control List #5

Background Information: An organization is implementing a three-router WAN configuration with multiple user LANs. A network administrator writes a standard ACL on the New York router to block traffic from the user at 192.168.1.11 to the file server at 10.0.1.82, while still permitting all other users from that network. The user is not able to connect to the file server but is also unable to connect to users on the 172.16.100.0/25 user LAN. No other networking issues have been reported to the helpdesk.

Task: Use the output from the troubleshooting commands provided to identify the configuration error.

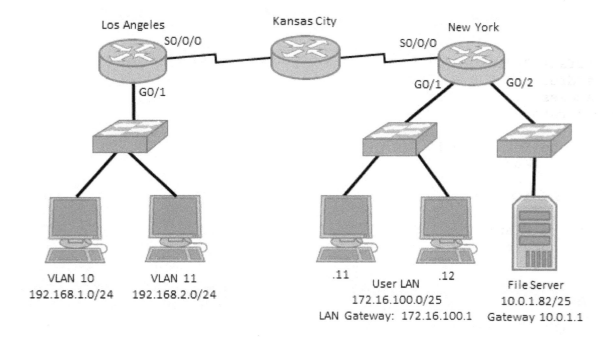

```
NewYork#show access-lists
Standard IP access list 90
    10 deny host 192.168.1.11
    20 permit any
```

```
NewYork#show running-config
Building configuration...

Current configuration : 1050 bytes
!
version 15.1
no service timestamps log datetime msec
no service timestamps debug datetime msec
no service password-encryption
!
hostname NewYork
!
interface GigabitEthernet0/0
no ip address
```

```
duplex auto
speed auto
shutdown
!
interface GigabitEthernet0/1
ip address 172.16.100.1 255.255.255.128
duplex auto
speed auto
!
interface GigabitEthernet0/2
ip address 10.0.1.1 255.255.255.128
duplex auto
speed auto
!
interface Serial0/0/0
ip address 10.0.0.6 255.255.255.252
ip access-group 90 in
clock rate 64000
!
interface Serial0/0/1
no ip address
clock rate 2000000
shutdown
!
interface Vlan1
no ip address
shutdown
!
router rip
version 2
network 10.0.0.0
network 172.16.0.0
no auto-summary
!
access-list 90 deny host 192.168.1.11
access-list 90 permit any
!
end
```

EXERCISE #17 – Troubleshooting a Standard Access Control List #6

Background Information: An organization is implementing a two-router WAN configuration with multiple user LANs. A network administrator writes a standard ACL on the New York router to block traffic from the user at 192.168.2.6 to the file server at 10.0.1.82, while still permitting all other users to access the file server. After implementing the standard ACL, other users are reporting that they are unable to access the file server.

Task: Use the output from the troubleshooting commands provided to identify the configuration error.

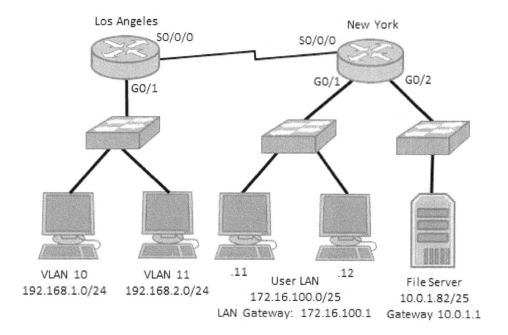

```
NewYork#show access-lists
Standard IP access list BlockDot6
     10 deny 192.168.2.6 0.0.0.0
     20 permit any


NewYork#show running-config
Building configuration...

Current configuration : 1050 bytes
!
version 15.1
no service timestamps log datetime msec
no service timestamps debug datetime msec
no service password-encryption
!
hostname NewYork
!
interface GigabitEthernet0/0
no ip address
```

```
duplex auto
speed auto
shutdown
!
interface GigabitEthernet0/1
ip address 172.16.100.1 255.255.255.128
duplex auto
speed auto
!
interface GigabitEthernet0/2
ip address 10.0.1.1 255.255.255.128
ip access-group BlockDot6 out
duplex auto
speed auto
shutdown
!
interface Serial0/0/0
ip address 10.0.0.6 255.255.255.252
clock rate 64000
!
interface Serial0/0/1
no ip address
clock rate 2000000
shutdown
!
interface Vlan1
no ip address
shutdown
!
router rip
version 2
network 10.0.0.0
network 172.16.0.0
no auto-summary
!
ip access-list standard BlockDot6
deny host 192.168.2.6
permit any
!
end
```

EXERCISE #18 – Troubleshooting a Standard Access Control List #7

Background Information: An organization is implementing a three-router WAN configuration with multiple user LANs. A network administrator writes a standard ACL on the New York router to block traffic from the user at 172.16.100.11 to the file server at 10.0.1.82, while still permitting all other users to access the file server. After implementing the standard ACL, other users are reporting that they are unable to access the file server.

Task: Use the output from the troubleshooting commands provided to identify the configuration error.

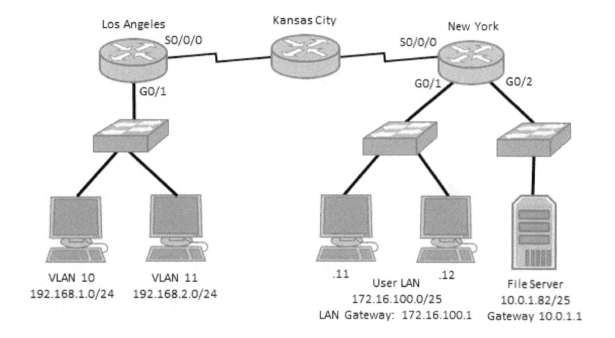

```
NewYork#show access-lists
Standard IP access list 1
      10 deny host 172.16.100.11


NewYork#show running-config
Building configuration...

Current configuration : 1050 bytes
!
version 15.1
no service timestamps log datetime msec
no service timestamps debug datetime msec
no service password-encryption
!
hostname NewYork
!
interface GigabitEthernet0/0
no ip address
duplex auto
```

```
speed auto
shutdown
!
interface GigabitEthernet0/1
ip address 172.16.100.1 255.255.255.128
duplex auto
speed auto
!
interface GigabitEthernet0/2
ip address 10.0.1.1 255.255.255.128
ip access-group 1 out
duplex auto
speed auto
!
interface Serial0/0/0
ip address 10.0.0.6 255.255.255.252
clock rate 64000
!
interface Serial0/0/1
no ip address
clock rate 2000000
shutdown
!
interface Vlan1
no ip address
shutdown
!
router rip
version 2
network 10.0.0.0
network 172.16.0.0
no auto-summary
!
access-list 1 deny host 172.16.100.11
!
end
```

EXERCISE #19 – Troubleshooting a Standard Access Control List #8

Background Information: Two routers serving two different buildings on a corporate campus are connected via an Ethernet connection. A network administrator writes a standard ACL on the Building2Rtr router to block traffic from the user at 192.168.100.11 to the file server at 10.0.1.15, while still permitting all other users from that network, however the user is still able to access the file server. No other networking issues have been reported to the helpdesk.

Task: Use the output from the troubleshooting commands provided to identify the configuration error.

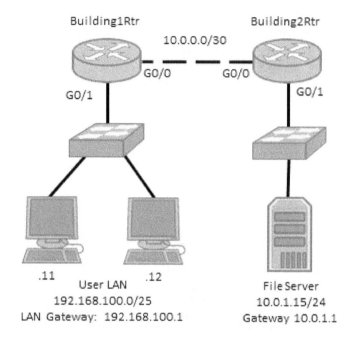

```
Building2Rtr#show access-lists
Standard IP access list BlockDot11
    10 deny host 192.168.100.11
    20 permit 192.168.100.0 0.0.0.127


Building2Rtr#show ip interface g0/0
GigabitEthernet0/0 is up, line protocol is up (connected)
    Internet address is 10.0.0.2/30
    Broadcast address is 255.255.255.255
    Address determined by setup command
    MTU is 1500 bytes
    Helper address is not set
    Directed broadcast forwarding is disabled
    Outgoing access list is not set
    Inbound access list is not set
    Proxy ARP is enabled
    Security level is default
    Split horizon is enabled
```

Building2Rtr#show ip interface g0/1
GigabitEthernet0/1 is up, line protocol is up (connected)
    Internet address is 10.0.1.1/24
    Broadcast address is 255.255.255.255
    Address determined by setup command
    MTU is 1500 bytes
    Helper address is not set
    Directed broadcast forwarding is disabled
    Outgoing access list is not set
    Inbound access list is not set
    Proxy ARP is enabled
    Security level is default
    Split horizon is enabled

SOLUTIONS TO EXERCISES FOR CHAPTER 3

SOLUTION - EXERCISE #12

The ACL is correctly applied outbound on Building2Rtr's G0/1 interface (as shown in the *show ip interface g0/1* command output); however, the ACL itself is not written correctly. As written, the ACL permits the entire 192.168.100.0/25 network (on line 10) before it denies the user at .11 of the same network (on line 20), so the ACL never runs this entry denying this user, and therefore the user's traffic is permitted. Keep in mind the rule regarding all ACLs – they work line by line and go with the first line that matches the traffic they are assessing. Once they find a match, they do not proceed further down the list of ACL entries. To correct the issue at this point, the network administrator could edit the ACL by issuing the *Building2Rtr(config)#ip access-list standard BlockDot11* command and adjusting the ACL to deny the user at .11 first. However, an ACL that is this short in length will probably be easier to delete and rebuild.

SOLUTION - EXERCISE #13

In this exercise, the standard ACL BlockDot11 is written correctly. Unfortunately, it is applied to the incorrect interface. It is applied in the outbound direction on interface G0/1, but it should be applied in an outbound direction on interface G0/2. The running configuration confirms that there is no ACL applied to either S0/0/0 or G0/2, which are the two interfaces on the New York router that the host will go through to get to the file server. The result of this configuration is that the host will be unable to connect to any resources on the 172.16.100.0/25 network.

SOLUTION - EXERCISE #14

In this exercise, the ACL BlockDot11 is applied to the correct interface, and in the correct direction, however the ACL is written incorrectly. As written, the ACL is denying host 192.168.11.11, not the correct host address of 192.168.1.11. The result is that the actual host of 192.168.1.11 will be permitted via the second line of the ACL (line 20.)

SOLUTION - EXERCISE #15

Here the ACL is written correctly and placed on the correct interface, but it is applied in the wrong direction. The line *ip access-group BlockDot12 in* only blocks traffic coming into the New York router from interface G0/2, which would not block any traffic generated from host 172.16.100.12. The administrator should make an adjustment to apply the same ACL to the same interface in an outbound direction instead.

SOLUTION - EXERCISE #16

In this exercise, the ACL is written correctly, but is placed on the Serial0/0/0 interface in the inbound direction to the router. Because of this placement, all traffic coming from host 192.168.1.11 will be blocked prior to entering the New York router, regardless of destination. That means that any traffic from that host to the 172.16.100.0/25 network would be blocked as well, which is the problem described in the background information. When using a standard ACL as this one is written, the best placement for the ACL would be on interface G0/2, thereby following the general rule of placing standard ACLs as close to the destination as possible.

SOLUTION - EXERCISE #17

If you are unable to find the error in the ACL here, don't worry. In this exercise, we see an example of how basic configuration settings can affect an otherwise correct and functional ACL. In this example, the ACL is written correctly and placed on the correct interface and in the correct direction. However, the G0/2 interface is in a down state for some reason (note the shutdown status of G0/2 listed in the *show running-config* output.) That is the cause of other users reporting an inability to access the file server.

SOLUTION - EXERCISE #18

This exercise shows an example of a common error when writing a standard ACL. Notice that the ACL only has one access control entry, which is denying the correct host address. Keep in mind that all ACLs have an invisible implicit deny at the end of the ACL, which will deny all traffic that is not explicitly permitted. Since the one line in the ACL is not followed by a permit line of any kind, the implicit deny comes into play, which therefore denies all other traffic. The result of this ACL is that all traffic, of any kind and from any source, will be completely blocked at the G0/2 interface in the outbound direction.

SOLUTION - EXERCISE #19

The ACL is written correctly, however the *show ip interface* commands reveal that the ACL was not applied to either of the interfaces on the Building2Rtr, given the output *Outgoing access list is not set, Inbound access list is not set* in both show commands. Note that the ACL does appropriately deny the .11 host before permitting the .0 network, and the 0.0.0.127 wildcard mask is correct for a /25 network. In this exercise, we could place the ACL on any interface. Best practice would be to set a standard ACL as close to the destination as possible, i.e. the G0/1 interface of Building2Rtr in the outbound direction.

CHAPTER 4: DHCP

Dynamic Host Configuration Protocol (DHCP) can be configured on Cisco routers, which is a reasonable solution for host addressing in a smaller network if enterprise DHCP service is not available. For the CCENT exam, you'll need to be familiar with the following troubleshooting topics related to DHCP (and DNS, which is issued to hosts via DHCP):

4.2 Troubleshoot client connectivity issues involving DNS.
4.4 Troubleshoot client- and router-based DHCP connectivity issues

Expect questions regarding DHCP to focus on one or more of the following issues:

1. Incorrectly excluded addresses related to the DHCP pool.
2. Incorrectly defined DHCP pool.
3. Client devices not correctly requesting DHCP service.
4. Incorrectly configured DHCP relay.
5. Incorrectly spelled DHCP pool, including variations in capitalization.

To troubleshoot these issues, there are several show commands you are expected to know and use, in addition to the *show running-config* command, which does provide nearly all the detail regarding DHCP that is needed. The DHCP-related show commands that are needed for the CCENT are:

show ip dhcp binding / show ipv6 dhcp binding

When run from the router that is set up as a DHCP server, the *show ip dhcp binding* command shows the IP addresses that have been issued through the DHCP service and the client MAC addresses that are using those addresses, which is called binding. Use this command to see all of the addresses in the DHCP pools that are leased out and in use.

show ip dhcp conflict

The *show ip dhcp conflict* command will show any addressing conflicts that the router is noticing and how the router learned about these conflicts. Use this command to troubleshoot DHCP if addressing appears to be conflicted or if changes have been made, including on the host devices.

show ip dhcp pool / show ipv6 dhcp pool

The *show ip dhcp pool* command is a very useful command that shows the address pool or pools that DHCP is configured to use and how many addresses are leased out. The *show running-config* command will verify the pool information as well, but will not give you the number of leased addresses.

show ip dhcp server statistics

The *show ip dhcp server statistics* command lists the count of messages that are sent and received by the DHCP router. Use this command to verify that DHCP messages are being sent and received, which is an indicator that the service is functioning correctly.

debug ip dhcp server events

The *debug ip dhcp server events* command is a debug command that will report out important dhcp server events, such as ip address assignments or updates to the dhcp database. To discontinue debugging, enter the *undebug all* command.

debug ipv6 dhcp detail

The debug ipv6 dhcp detail command is a debug command that verifies the receipt and transmission of DHCPv6 messages. To discontinue debugging, enter the *undebug all* command.

EXERCISE #20 – Troubleshooting Dynamic Host Configuration Protocol #1

Background Information: An organization has a two-building network and would like to configure DHCP on the Building2Rtr router. This configuration needs to serve IP addresses to the user LANs in both building 1 and building 2. The network administrator has configured DHCP on the Building2Rtr router, but hosts on the 172.16.1.0/24 network are reporting that they are unable to acquire an IP address.

Task: Use the output from the troubleshooting commands provided to identify the configuration error.

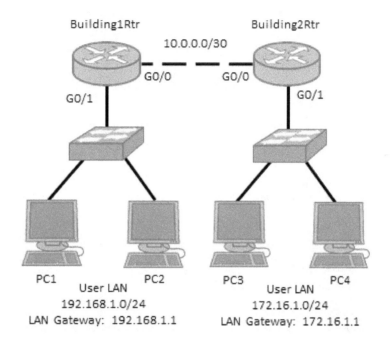

```
Command Prompt – PC3

C:\>ipconfig

Autoconfiguration IP Address....: 169.254.203.96
Subnet Mask....................: 255.255.0.0
Default Gateway.................: 0.0.0.0
```

Building2Rtr#show ip dhcp binding
```
IP address        Client-ID/              Lease expiration Type
                  Hardware address
192.168.1.2       FFAA.2BC0.A42A          --               Automatic
192.168.1.3       FFAA.CFB7.C069          --               Automatic
```

Building2Rtr#show running-config
```
Building configuration...

Current configuration : 1038 bytes
```

```
!
version 15.1
no service timestamps log datetime msec
no service timestamps debug datetime msec
no service password-encryption
!
hostname Building2Rtr
!
ip dhcp excluded-address 192.168.1.1
ip dhcp excluded-address 172.16.1.1
!
ip dhcp pool UserLAN1
network 192.168.1.0 255.255.255.0
default-router 192.168.1.1
!
interface GigabitEthernet0/0
ip address 10.0.0.2 255.255.255.252
duplex auto
speed auto
!
interface GigabitEthernet0/1
ip address 172.16.1.1 255.255.255.0
duplex auto
speed auto
!
interface GigabitEthernet0/2
no ip address
duplex auto
speed auto
shutdown
!
interface Vlan1
no ip address
shutdown
!
router rip
version 2
network 10.0.0.0
network 172.16.0.0
no auto-summary
!
end
```

EXERCISE #21 – Troubleshooting Dynamic Host Configuration Protocol #2

Background Information: An organization has a two-building network and would like to configure DHCP on the Building2Rtr router. This configuration needs to serve IP addresses to the user LANs in both building 1 and building 2. The network administrator has configured DHCP on the Building2Rtr router but the host on the 172.16.1.0/24 network is unable to connect to resources outside of their LAN.

Task: Use the output from the troubleshooting commands provided to identify the configuration error.

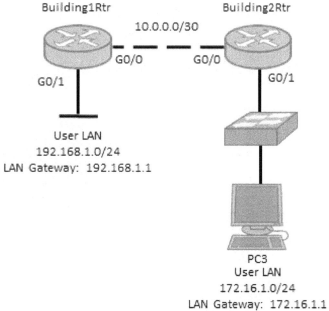

Command Prompt – PC3

```
C:\>ipconfig

IP Address.........................: 172.16.1.2
Subnet Mask.....................: 255.255.255.0
Default Gateway................: 0.0.0.0

C:\>ping 10.0.0.2

Pinging 10.0.0.2 with 32 bytes of data:

Request timed out.
Request timed out.
Request timed out.
Request timed out.
```

Building2Rtr#show running-config
Building configuration...

```
Current configuration : 1038 bytes
!
version 15.1
no service timestamps log datetime msec
no service timestamps debug datetime msec
no service password-encryption
!
hostname Building2Rtr
!
ip dhcp excluded-address 192.168.1.1
ip dhcp excluded-address 172.16.1.1
!
ip dhcp pool UserLAN1
network 192.168.1.0 255.255.255.0
default-router 192.168.1.1
ip dhcp pool UserLAN2
network 172.16.1.0 255.255.255.0
!
interface GigabitEthernet0/0
ip address 10.0.0.2 255.255.255.252
duplex auto
speed auto
!
interface GigabitEthernet0/1
ip address 172.16.1.1 255.255.255.0
duplex auto
speed auto
!
interface GigabitEthernet0/2
no ip address
duplex auto
speed auto
shutdown
!
interface Vlan1
no ip address
shutdown
!
router rip
version 2
network 10.0.0.0
network 172.16.0.0
no auto-summary
!
end
```

EXERCISE #22 – Troubleshooting Dynamic Host Configuration Protocol #3

Background Information: An organization has a two-building network and would like to configure DHCP on the Building2Rtr router. This configuration needs to serve IP addresses to the user LANs in both building 1 and building 2. The network administrator has configured DHCP on the Building2Rtr router but hosts on the 192.168.1.0/24 network are unable to obtain IP addresses.

Task: Use the output from the troubleshooting commands provided to identify the configuration error.

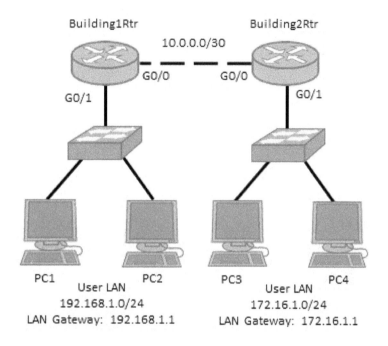

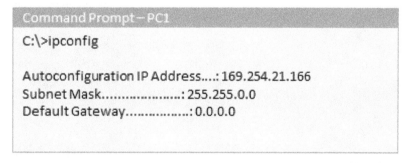

```
Building2Rtr#show running-config
Building configuration...

Current configuration : 1038 bytes
!
version 15.1
no service timestamps log datetime msec
no service timestamps debug datetime msec
no service password-encryption
!
hostname Building2Rtr
```

```
!
ip dhcp excluded-address 192.168.1.1
ip dhcp excluded-address 172.16.1.1
!
ip dhcp pool UserLAN1
network 192.168.1.0 255.255.255.0
default-router 192.168.1.1
ip dhcp pool UserLAN2
network 172.16.1.0 255.255.255.0
default-router 172.16.1.1
!
interface GigabitEthernet0/0
ip address 10.0.0.2 255.255.255.252
duplex auto
speed auto
!
interface GigabitEthernet0/1
ip address 172.16.1.1 255.255.255.0
duplex auto
speed auto
!
interface GigabitEthernet0/2
no ip address
duplex auto
speed auto
shutdown
!
interface Vlan1
no ip address
shutdown
!
router rip
version 2
network 10.0.0.0
network 172.16.0.0
no auto-summary
!
end
```

Building1Rtr#show running-config
```
Building configuration...

Current configuration : 827 bytes
!
version 15.1
no service timestamps log datetime msec
no service timestamps debug datetime msec
no service password-encryption
!
hostname Building1Rtr
!
interface GigabitEthernet0/0
```

```
ip address 10.0.0.1 255.255.255.252
duplex auto
speed auto
!
interface GigabitEthernet0/1
ip address 192.168.1.1 255.255.255.0
ip helper-address 10.0.0.1
duplex auto
speed auto
!
interface GigabitEthernet0/2
no ip address
duplex auto
speed auto
shutdown
!
interface Vlan1
no ip address
shutdown
!
router rip
version 2
network 10.0.0.0
network 192.168.1.0
no auto-summary
!
end
```

EXERCISE #23 – Troubleshooting Dynamic Host Configuration Protocol #4

Background Information: An organization has a two-building network and would like to configure DHCP on the Building2Rtr router. This configuration needs to serve IP addresses to the user LANs in both building 1 and building 2. The network administrator has configured DHCP on the Building2Rtr router but hosts on the 192.168.1.0/24 network are unable to obtain IP addresses.

Task: Use the output from the troubleshooting commands provided to identify the configuration error.

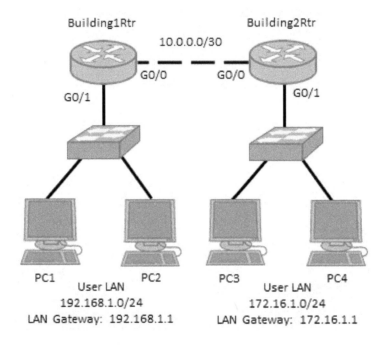

Building1Rtr   Building2Rtr
                    10.0.0.0/30
            G0/0   G0/0
G0/1   G0/1

PC1   PC2   PC3   PC4
     User LAN   User LAN
   192.168.1.0/24   172.16.1.0/24
LAN Gateway: 192.168.1.1   LAN Gateway: 172.16.1.1

```
Command Prompt – PC1

C:\>ipconfig

Autoconfiguration IP Address....: 169.254.21.166
Subnet Mask.....................: 255.255.0.0
Default Gateway.................: 0.0.0.0
```

```
Building2Rtr#show running-config
Building configuration...

Current configuration : 1038 bytes
!
version 15.1
no service timestamps log datetime msec
no service timestamps debug datetime msec
no service password-encryption
!
hostname Building2Rtr
```

```
!
ip dhcp excluded-address 192.168.1.1
ip dhcp excluded-address 172.16.1.1
!
ip dhcp pool UserLAN1
network 192.168.1.0 255.255.255.0
default-router 192.168.1.1
ip dhcp pool UserLAN2
network 172.16.1.0 255.255.255.0
default-router 172.16.1.1
!
interface GigabitEthernet0/0
ip address 10.0.0.2 255.255.255.252
duplex auto
speed auto
!
interface GigabitEthernet0/1
ip address 172.16.1.1 255.255.255.0
duplex auto
speed auto
!
interface GigabitEthernet0/2
no ip address
duplex auto
speed auto
shutdown
!
interface Vlan1
no ip address
shutdown
!
router rip
version 2
network 10.0.0.0
network 172.16.0.0
no auto-summary
!
end
```

Building1Rtr#show running-config
```
Building configuration...

Current configuration : 827 bytes
!
version 15.1
no service timestamps log datetime msec
no service timestamps debug datetime msec
no service password-encryption
!
hostname Building1Rtr
!
interface GigabitEthernet0/0
```

```
ip address 10.0.0.1 255.255.255.252
ip helper-address 10.0.0.2
duplex auto
speed auto
!
interface GigabitEthernet0/1
ip address 192.168.1.1 255.255.255.0
duplex auto
speed auto
!
interface GigabitEthernet0/2
no ip address
duplex auto
speed auto
shutdown
!
interface Vlan1
no ip address
shutdown
!
router rip
version 2
network 10.0.0.0
network 192.168.1.0
no auto-summary
!
end
```

EXERCISE #24 – Troubleshooting Dynamic Host Configuration Protocol #5

Background Information: An organization has a two-building network and would like to configure DHCP on the Building2Rtr router. This configuration needs to serve IP addresses to the user LANs in both building 1 and building 2. The network administrator has configured DHCP on the Building2Rtr router but hosts on the 172.16.1.0/24 network are unable to connect to resources outside of their LAN.

Task: Use the output from the troubleshooting commands provided to identify the configuration error.

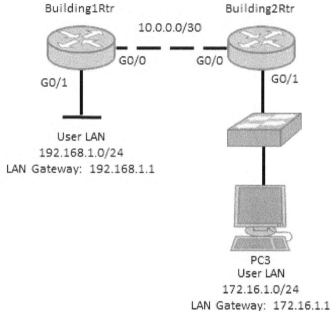

```
Command Prompt – PC3

C:\>ipconfig

IP Address.....................: 172.16.1.2
Subnet Mask....................: 255.255.255.0
Default Gateway................: 0.0.0.0

C:\>ping 10.0.0.2

Pinging 10.0.0.2 with 32 bytes of data:

Request timed out.
Request timed out.
Request timed out.
Request timed out.
```

Building2Rtr#show running-config
Building configuration...

```
Current configuration : 1038 bytes
!
version 15.1
no service timestamps log datetime msec
no service timestamps debug datetime msec
no service password-encryption
!
hostname Building2Rtr
!
ip dhcp excluded-address 192.168.1.1
ip dhcp excluded-address 172.16.1.1
!
ip dhcp pool UserLAN1
network 192.168.1.0 255.255.255.0
default-router 192.168.1.1
ip dhcp pool UserLAN2
network 172.16.1.0 255.255.255.0
ip dhcp pool userLAN2
default-router 172.16.1.1
!
interface GigabitEthernet0/0
ip address 10.0.0.2 255.255.255.252
duplex auto
speed auto
!
interface GigabitEthernet0/1
ip address 172.16.1.1 255.255.255.0
duplex auto
speed auto
!
interface GigabitEthernet0/2
no ip address
duplex auto
speed auto
shutdown
!
interface Vlan1
no ip address
shutdown
!
router rip
version 2
network 10.0.0.0
network 172.16.0.0
no auto-summary
!
End
```

Building1Rtr#show running-config
```
Building configuration...

Current configuration : 827 bytes
```

```
!
version 15.1
no service timestamps log datetime msec
no service timestamps debug datetime msec
no service password-encryption
!
hostname Building1Rtr
!
interface GigabitEthernet0/0
ip address 10.0.0.1 255.255.255.252
duplex auto
speed auto
!
interface GigabitEthernet0/1
ip address 192.168.1.1 255.255.255.0
ip helper-address 10.0.0.2
duplex auto
speed auto
!
interface GigabitEthernet0/2
no ip address
duplex auto
speed auto
shutdown
!
interface Vlan1
no ip address
shutdown
!
router rip
version 2
network 10.0.0.0
network 192.168.1.0
no auto-summary
!
end
```

EXERCISE #25 – Troubleshooting Dynamic Host Configuration Protocol #6

Background Information: An organization has a two-building network and would like to configure DHCP on the Building2Rtr router. This configuration needs to serve IP addresses to the user LANs in both building 1 and building 2. The network administrator has configured DHCP on the Building2Rtr router but hosts on the 172.16.1.0/24 network are unable to acquire an IP address.

Task: Use the output from the troubleshooting commands provided to identify the configuration error.

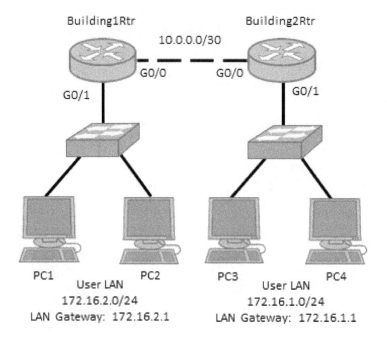

```
Command Prompt – PC3

C:\>ipconfig

Autoconfiguration IP Address....: 169.254.203.96
Subnet Mask......................: 255.255.0.0
Default Gateway..................: 0.0.0.0
```

```
Building2Rtr#show ip dhcp pool

Pool UserLAN1 :
Total addresses : 254
Leased addresses : 2
Excluded addresses : 2

1 subnet is currently in the pool
Current index      IP address range                Leased/Excluded/Total
172.16.2.1         172.16.2.1 - 172.16.2.254       2 / 2 / 254
```

```
Pool UserLAN2 :
Total addresses : 254
Leased addresses : 0
Excluded addresses : 2

1 subnet is currently in the pool
Current index      IP address range                 Leased/Excluded/Total
172.16.1.1         172.16.1.1 - 172.16.1.254        0 / 2 / 254
```

Building2Rtr#show running-config
```
Building configuration...

Current configuration : 1038 bytes
!
version 15.1
no service timestamps log datetime msec
no service timestamps debug datetime msec
no service password-encryption
!
hostname Building2Rtr
!
ip dhcp excluded-address 172.16.2.1
ip dhcp excluded-address 172.16.1.1
!
ip dhcp pool UserLAN1
network 172.16.2.0 255.255.255.0
default-router 172.16.2.1
ip dhcp pool UserLAN2
network 172.16.3.0 255.255.255.0
default-router 172.16.3.1
!
interface GigabitEthernet0/0
ip address 10.0.0.2 255.255.255.252
duplex auto
speed auto
!
interface GigabitEthernet0/1
ip address 172.16.1.1 255.255.255.0
duplex auto
speed auto
!
interface GigabitEthernet0/2
no ip address
duplex auto
speed auto
shutdown
!
interface Vlan1
no ip address
shutdown
!
router rip
```

```
version 2
network 10.0.0.0
network 172.16.0.0
no auto-summary
!
end
```

EXERCISE #26 – Troubleshooting Dynamic Host Configuration Protocol #7

Background Information: An organization has a two-building network with DHCP installed on the Building2Rtr router. They also have a DNS server connected to the router. DHCP is responsible for sharing the DNS server information with all hosts, but users on the 172.16.1.0/24 network are unable to resolve domain names. After investigating, a network administrator has determined that users on the 172.16.1.0 user LAN can ping the DNS server, but cannot resolve domain names.

Task: Use the output from the troubleshooting commands provided to identify the configuration error.

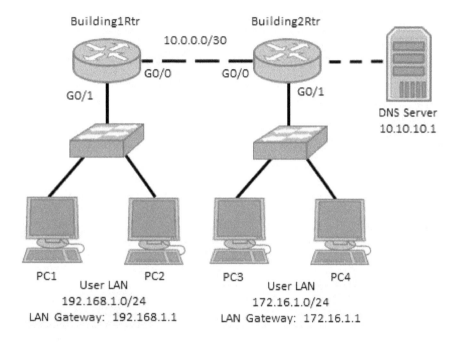

```
Building2Rtr#show running-config
Building configuration...

Current configuration : 1038 bytes
!
version 15.1
no service timestamps log datetime msec
no service timestamps debug datetime msec
no service password-encryption
!
hostname Building2Rtr
!
ip dhcp excluded-address 192.168.1.1
ip dhcp excluded-address 172.16.1.1
!
ip dhcp pool UserLAN1
network 192.168.1.0 255.255.255.0
default-router 192.168.1.1
dns-server 10.10.10.1
ip dhcp pool UserLAN2
```

```
network 172.16.1.0 255.255.255.0
default-router 172.16.1.1
!
interface GigabitEthernet0/0
ip address 10.0.0.2 255.255.255.252
duplex auto
speed auto
!
interface GigabitEthernet0/1
ip address 172.16.1.1 255.255.255.0
duplex auto
speed auto
!
interface GigabitEthernet0/2
ip address 10.10.10.2 255.255.255.0
duplex auto
speed auto
!
interface Vlan1
no ip address
shutdown
!
router rip
version 2
network 10.0.0.0
network 172.16.0.0
no auto-summary
!
end
```

EXERCISE #27 – Troubleshooting Dynamic Host Configuration Protocol #8

Background Information: An organization has a two-building network with DHCP installed on the Building2Rtr router. They also have a DNS server connected to the router. The network administrators are using DHCP to share DNS information with clients on the Building2Rtr user LAN, as well as provide IPv4 addresses. You have received a help desk call from an employee on the Building2Rtr user LAN complaining that he cannot connect to the internet.

Task: Use the output from the troubleshooting commands provided to identify the configuration error.

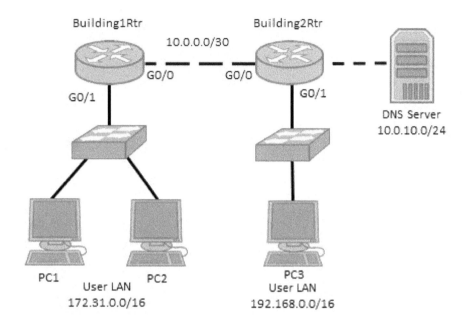

```
Building2Rtr#show running-config
Building configuration...

Current configuration : 931 bytes
!
version 15.1
no service timestamps log datetime msec
no service timestamps debug datetime msec
no service password-encryption
!
hostname Building2Rtr
!
ip cef
!
no ipv6 cef
!
ip dhcp pool UserLAN1
network 192.168.1.0 255.255.255.0
default-router 192.168.1.1
dns-server 10.0.10.10
!
interface GigabitEthernet0/0
```

```
ip address 10.0.0.2 255.255.255.252
duplex auto
speed auto
!
interface GigabitEthernet0/1
ip address 192.168.0.1 255.255.0.0
duplex auto
speed auto
!
interface GigabitEthernet0/2
ip address 10.0.10.1 255.255.255.0
duplex auto
speed auto
!
interface Vlan1
no ip address
shutdown
!
ip classless
!
ip flow-export version 9
!
ip route 0.0.0.0 0.0.0.0 GigabitEthernet0/0
!
end
```

SOLUTIONS TO EXERCISES FOR CHAPTER 4

SOLUTION - EXERCISE #20

In this exercise, we can confirm that the router has not issued any addresses to the 172.16.1.0/24 network by viewing the *show ip dhcp binding* command output on the Building2Rtr router. Interestingly, we can also confirm that the router has issued addresses to the 192.168.1.0/24 network. When we view the *show running-config* command issued we see that an address pool for the 172.16.1.0 network has not been created. Since the router will not issue addresses for a pool that doesn't exist, local devices on that network will either self-configure an APIPA address or need to have a static address assigned, which is what we saw in the command prompt output for PC3. APIPA is Automatic Private IP Addressing and is a Microsoft Windows feature that configures an address in the 169.254.0.0/16 address range, which is intended to be non-routable.

SOLUTION - EXERCISE #21

In this exercise, a look at the *show running-config* verifies that the UserLAN2 pool, which is set up to serve the 172.16.1.0/24 network, has not been issued the *default-router* command, and therefore isn't providing any hosts on that network with a gateway configuration. This is confirmed with the command prompt output from PC3, which shows that the default gateway has not been set and is reverting to a default address of 0.0.0.0, and that a ping attempt out of the network has failed. Because the devices on this LAN segment can still be configured with an address and subnet mask via DHCP, but not a gateway, they will be able to get an IP address but will not be able to send traffic off their local LAN.

SOLUTION - EXERCISE #22

In this exercise, we look at both routers to determine why the 192.168.1.0 network hosts are unable to acquire DHCP-issued addresses. We start with confirmation that PC1 is assigned an APIPA address, and therefore is not communicating with a DHCP server (APIPA is Automatic Private IP Addressing and is a Microsoft Windows feature that configures an address in the 169.254.0.0/16 address range, which is intended to be non-routable.) The Building2Rtr *show running-config* output confirms that this router is acting as a DHCP server, and the service is correctly configured. The Building1Rtr configuration is the culprit, as the ip helper-address is incorrectly assigned the address of 10.0.0.1. When setting up this relay service, there are two important factors to consider. First, the *ip helper-address* command must be placed on the interface or interfaces that will *receive* the initial DHCP discover broadcast message from the host – in other words – the host's gateway interface. Second, the *ip helper-address* command must point to the router that is providing the DHCP service. In this example, we can confirm from the *show running-config* outputs that 10.0.0.1 is not an address on the Building2Rtr router, and therefore the DHCP messages will never be delivered to that router as necessary.

SOLUTION - EXERCISE #23

In this exercise, the *ip helper-address* command is written correctly, with the correct IP address, but it is applied to the wrong interface – G0/0. Since interface G0/0 will never receive an inbound DHCP discover packet from hosts on the 192.168.1.0/24 network, that *ip helper-address* command cannot assist in providing those hosts with DHCP service. The command instead needs to be applied to the G0/1 interface.

SOLUTION - EXERCISE #24

The *show running-config* command output shows us that there are three separate DHCP pools, and that the configuration for the 172.16.1.0 network is split between two of the pools. DHCP pools, like many other items within the Cisco IOS, are case-sensitive. The router is interpreting this as three separate pools because of the variation in capitalization. An error like this is common when a pool is established, and then is modified later. When this occurs, often the network administrator will spell the pool in a different way the second time, and instead of editing the first pool, they are creating a second and distinct pool. The best practice here is to always verify your input via the *show running-config* command before and after your adjustments.

SOLUTION - EXERCISE #25

In this exercise, the 172.16.1.0/24 network hosts are unable to obtain a DHCP address. We can see from the command prompt of PC3 that an *ipconfig* command issued on that host resulted in an Automatic Private IP Address, or APIPA address being assigned locally on the device. When we see an APIPA address on a host, it can be considered verification that the host attempted and was unsuccessful at obtaining an address via the DHCP protocol. In the *show ip dhcp pool* and in the *show running-config* commands issued on the Building2Rtr router, we can see that the UserLAN2 pool was given an incorrect pool of 172.16.3.0/24. Since this is a mismatch with interface G0/1's IP address of 172.16.1.1 on the router, the router is unable to resolve DHCP requests that arrive on that interface.

SOLUTION - EXERCISE #26

In this exercise, the 172.16.1.0/24 network hosts are unable to resolve domain names but can ping the DNS server. They can ping the server because their gateway router is able to route them to the address of the DNS server, as both networks are directly connected, and routing connectivity and DNS service are independent. We can see from the *show running-config* command output that a simple error was made in the configuration – the DNS server settings were applied to the 192.168.1.0 network, but not the 172.16.1.0 network.

SOLUTION - EXERCISE #27

This is an example of DHCP relying on correct IPv4 subnetting. In this exercise, the Building2Rtr user LAN is on the 192.168.0.0/16 and has a default gateway of 192.168.0.1, which is correctly configured on interface G0/1 as shown in the *show running-config*. The DHCP pool is set to 192.168.1.0/24 and a gateway of 192.168.1.1, which is a completely different subnetwork. In this example, users will not be able to acquire any DHCP-issued information, including the DNS server address.

CHAPTER 5: Switch and VLAN Configuration

Proper switch configuration is critical in any network setup, as switches operate at the access layer of our network and therefore provide access to the network for all users. Because switches are the point of contact between the user and the network, they are a primary target of malicious attack and therefore a focus of security procedures. In this chapter, we will look at the switch-related troubleshooting topics covered on the CCENT exam, including VLANs and inter-VLAN routing with router-on-a-stick. The exam objectives related to troubleshooting switches and layer 2 of the OSI model are:

2.4 Configure, verify, and troubleshoot VLANs (normal range) spanning multiple switches
- *2.4.a Access ports (data and voice)*
- *2.4.b Default VLAN*

2.5 Configure, verify, and troubleshoot interswitch connectivity
- *2.5.a Trunk ports*
- *2.5.b 802.1Q*
- *2.5.c Native VLAN*

2.7 Configure, verify, and troubleshoot port security
- *2.7.a Static*
- *2.7.b Dynamic*
- *2.7.c Sticky*
- *2.7.d Max MAC addresses*
- *2.7.e Violation actions*
- *2.7.f Err-disable recovery*

3.4 Configure, verify, and troubleshoot inter-VLAN routing
- *3.4.a Router on a stick*

You'll notice from the exam objectives that there is a great deal of content related to switch configuration and layer 2, including VLANs, trunking, port security, and router on a stick configuration.

While Cisco Discovery Protocol (CDP) is not specifically identified as a troubleshooting objective for the CCENT exam, it is a layer 2 protocol that, like Link Layer Discovery Protocol (LLDP), is included on the exam objectives in general. CDP and LLDP are layer 2 protocols that enable devices to discover configuration information about neighboring devices on a network. These protocols are beneficial for troubleshooting and network topology verification, and therefore the show commands related to these protocols have been included in this chapter.

You should expect switch and layer 2 exam questions to focus on one or more of the following issues:

1. Router on a stick is incorrectly configured, either through incorrect trunking or incorrect sub-interfaces on the router.
2. Port security is incorrectly configured on switch ports.
3. Trunk ports are incorrectly configured between switches.
4. VLANs are not defined, or appropriate ports have not been placed in the correct VLAN.
5. Switchports are in an error-disabled state due to port security.

The show commands related to these exam objectives are:

show mac-address-table

This command shows the mac address table on the switch and which addresses were learned on the ports of that switch, as well as which VLANs they are assigned to. Use this command to evaluate what the switch "knows" as far as host device location.

show port-security interface

The *show port-security interface* command displays the port-security information for the switch's ports. This information can also be found in the *show running-config* command output. Use the *show port-security interface* command when you need to verify if a specific port or ports are configured with port security.

show port-security address

The *show port-security address* command displays the secure MAC addresses that are recorded on the switch. Use this command to verify the MAC addresses that have been bound to specific ports.

show vlan / show vlan brief

The *show vlan* commands display the VLANs on a switch and the ports assigned to those VLANs. Use this command to verify the existence of VLANs and verify which VLAN a port has been placed in.

show interfaces *interface* switchport

This command verifies the switchport settings of a specific interface on the switch. This information can also be verified in the *show running-config* command output.

show interfaces switchport / show interfaces trunk

These commands show the switchport or trunk settings for an interface or interfaces. This information can also be verified in the *show running-config* command output.

show cdp neighbors

The *show cdp neighbors* displays a list of Cisco devices that are directly connected and learned through the CDP protocol. Use this protocol and command to reverse engineer or verify a network topology.

show cdp interface

This command displays the interfaces that are enabled with CDP on a device. Use this command to confirm CDP is operational on an interface, especially if you are not receiving CDP updates via that interface.

show lldp / show lldp neighbors

The *show lldp* and *show lldp neighbors* commands display a list of any devices that are directly connected and learned through the LLDP protocol. This is similar to the CDP protocol, but is not Cisco-proprietary.

EXERCISE #28 – Troubleshooting Switch and VLAN Configuration #1

Background Information: A new company has set up a basic router-on-a-stick network to serve two VLANs, which have been set up as VLAN 10 and VLAN 20. The technician has been unable to get the configuration to work and asks you for assistance.

Task: Use the output from the troubleshooting commands provided to identify the configuration error.

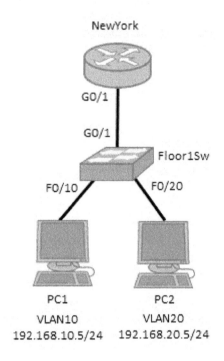

```
Command Prompt – PC1

C:\>ipconfig

IP Address.........................: 192.168.10.5
Subnet Mask.....................: 255.255.255.0
Default Gateway.................: 192.168.10.1

C:\>ping 192.168.20.5

Pinging 192.168.20.5 with 32 bytes of data:

Request timed out.
Request timed out.
Request timed out.
Request timed out.
```

```
NewYork#show running-config | begin interface
interface GigabitEthernet0/0
no ip address
duplex auto
speed auto
shutdown
!
interface GigabitEthernet0/1
no ip address
duplex auto
speed auto
!
interface GigabitEthernet0/1.10
encapsulation dot1Q 12
ip address 192.168.10.1 255.255.255.0
!
interface GigabitEthernet0/1.20
encapsulation dot1Q 20
ip address 192.168.20.1 255.255.255.0
!
interface GigabitEthernet0/2
no ip address
duplex auto
speed auto
shutdown
!
interface Vlan1
no ip address
shutdown
!
end
```

EXERCISE #29 – Troubleshooting Switch and VLAN Configuration #2

Background Information: A new company has set up a basic router-on-a-stick network to serve two VLANs, which have been set up as VLAN 10 and VLAN 20. The technician has been unable to get the configuration to work and asks you for assistance.

Task: Use the output from the troubleshooting commands provided to identify the configuration error.

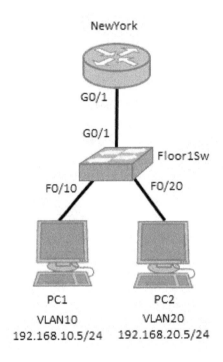

```
Command Prompt – PC1

C:\>ipconfig

IP Address.........................: 192.168.10.5
Subnet Mask.....................: 255.255.255.0
Default Gateway................: 192.168.10.1

C:\>ping 192.168.20.5

Pinging 192.168.20.5 with 32 bytes of data:

Request timed out.
Request timed out.
Request timed out.
Request timed out.
```

```
NewYork#show running-config | begin interface
interface GigabitEthernet0/0
no ip address
duplex auto
speed auto
shutdown
!
interface GigabitEthernet0/1
no ip address
duplex auto
speed auto
!
interface GigabitEthernet0/1.10
encapsulation dot1Q 10
ip address 192.168.10.1 255.255.255.0
!
interface GigabitEthernet0/1.20
encapsulation dot1Q 20
ip address 192.168.20.1 255.255.255.0
!
interface GigabitEthernet0/2
no ip address
duplex auto
speed auto
shutdown
!
interface Vlan1
no ip address
shutdown
!
end


Floor1Switch#show running-config
Building configuration...

Current configuration : 1244 bytes
!
version 12.2
!
hostname Floor1Switch
!
interface FastEthernet0/1
!
interface FastEthernet0/2
!
interface FastEthernet0/3
!
interface FastEthernet0/4
!
interface FastEthernet0/5
!
interface FastEthernet0/6
```

```
!
interface FastEthernet0/7
!
interface FastEthernet0/8
!
interface FastEthernet0/9
!
interface FastEthernet0/10
switchport access vlan 10
switchport mode trunk
!
interface FastEthernet0/11
!
interface FastEthernet0/12
!
interface FastEthernet0/13
!
interface FastEthernet0/14
!
interface FastEthernet0/15
!
interface FastEthernet0/16
!
interface FastEthernet0/17
!
interface FastEthernet0/18
!
interface FastEthernet0/19
!
interface FastEthernet0/20
switchport access vlan 20
switchport mode access
!
interface FastEthernet0/21
!
interface FastEthernet0/22
!
interface FastEthernet0/23
!
interface FastEthernet0/24
!
interface GigabitEthernet0/1
switchport trunk allowed vlan 10,20
switchport mode trunk
!
interface GigabitEthernet0/2
!
interface Vlan1
no ip address
shutdown
!
end
```

EXERCISE #30 – Troubleshooting Switch and VLAN Configuration #3

Background Information: A new company has set up a basic router-on-a-stick network to serve two VLANs, which have been set up as VLAN 10 and VLAN 20. They also have a file server connected to their network on its own subnetwork.   The technician has been unable to get the router-on-a-stick configuration to work and asks you for assistance.

Task: Use the output from the troubleshooting commands provided to identify the configuration error.

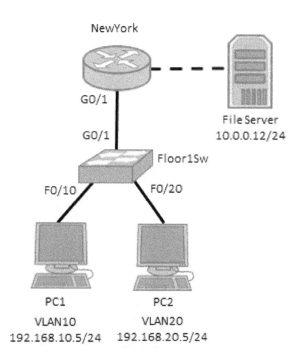

NewYork

GO/1

File Server
10.0.0.12/24

GO/1

Floor1Sw

FO/10   FO/20

PC1   PC2
VLAN10   VLAN20
192.168.10.5/24   192.168.20.5/24

Command Prompt – PC1

C:\>ipconfig

IP Address.........................: 192.168.10.5
Subnet Mask.....................: 255.255.255.0
Default Gateway................: 192.168.10.1

C:\>ping 192.168.20.5

Pinging 192.168.20.5 with 32 bytes of data:

Request timed out.
Request timed out.
Request timed out.
Request timed out.

Floor1Switch#show vlan brief

```
VLAN Name                             Status    Ports
---- -------------------- --------- -------------------------------
1    default                          active    Fa0/1, Fa0/2, Fa0/3, Fa0/4
                                                Fa0/5, Fa0/6, Fa0/7, Fa0/8
                                                Fa0/9, Fa0/11, Fa0/12, Fa0/13
                                                Fa0/14, Fa0/15, Fa0/16, Fa0/17
                                                Fa0/18, Fa0/19, Fa0/21, Fa0/22
                                                Fa0/23, Fa0/24, Gig0/2
10   VLAN0010                         active    Fa0/10
20   VLAN0020                         active    Fa0/20
```

NewYork#show running-config | begin interface

```
interface GigabitEthernet0/0
ip address 10.0.0.1 255.255.255.0
duplex auto
speed auto
!
interface GigabitEthernet0/1
no ip address
duplex auto
speed auto
!
interface GigabitEthernet0/1.20
encapsulation dot1Q 20
ip address 192.168.20.1 255.255.255.0
!
interface GigabitEthernet0/2
no ip address
duplex auto
speed auto
shutdown
!
interface Vlan1
no ip address
shutdown
!
end
```

Floor1Switch#show running-config

```
Building configuration...

Current configuration : 1244 bytes
!
version 12.2
!
hostname Floor1Switch
!
interface FastEthernet0/1
!
```

```
interface FastEthernet0/2
!
interface FastEthernet0/3
!
interface FastEthernet0/4
!
interface FastEthernet0/5
!
interface FastEthernet0/6
!
interface FastEthernet0/7
!
interface FastEthernet0/8
!
interface FastEthernet0/9
!
interface FastEthernet0/10
switchport access vlan 10
switchport mode access
!
interface FastEthernet0/11
!
interface FastEthernet0/12
!
interface FastEthernet0/13
!
interface FastEthernet0/14
!
interface FastEthernet0/15
!
interface FastEthernet0/16
!
interface FastEthernet0/17
!
interface FastEthernet0/18
!
interface FastEthernet0/19
!
interface FastEthernet0/20
switchport access vlan 20
switchport mode access
!
interface FastEthernet0/21
!
interface FastEthernet0/22
!
interface FastEthernet0/23
!
interface FastEthernet0/24
!
interface GigabitEthernet0/1
switchport trunk allowed vlan 10,20
switchport mode trunk
```

```
!
interface GigabitEthernet0/2
!
interface Vlan1
no ip address
shutdown
!
end
```

EXERCISE #31 – Troubleshooting Switch and VLAN Configuration #4

Background Information: A new company has set up a basic router-on-a-stick network to serve two VLANs, which have been set up as VLAN 10 and VLAN 20. They also have a file server connected to their network on its own subnetwork. The technician has been unable to get the router-on-a-stick configuration to work and asks you for assistance.

Task: Use the output from the troubleshooting commands provided to identify the configuration error.

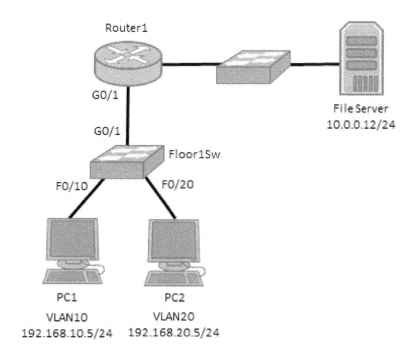

Command Prompt – PC1

C:\>ipconfig

IP Address.........................: 192.168.10.5
Subnet Mask.....................: 255.255.255.0
Default Gateway................: 192.168.10.1

C:\>ping 192.168.20.5

Pinging 192.168.20.5 with 32 bytes of data:

Request timed out.
Request timed out.
Request timed out.
Request timed out.

Floor1Switch#show vlan brief

```
VLAN Name                 Status    Ports
---- -------------------- --------- -------------------------------
1    default              active    Fa0/1, Fa0/2, Fa0/3, Fa0/4
                                    Fa0/5, Fa0/6, Fa0/7, Fa0/8
                                    Fa0/9, Fa0/11, Fa0/12, Fa0/13
                                    Fa0/14, Fa0/15, Fa0/16, Fa0/17
                                    Fa0/18, Fa0/19, Fa0/21, Fa0/22
                                    Fa0/23, Fa0/24, Gig0/1, Gig0/2
10   VLAN0010             active    Fa0/10
20   VLAN0020             active    Fa0/20
```

Router1#show running-config | begin interface
```
interface GigabitEthernet0/0
ip address 10.0.0.1 255.255.255.0
duplex auto
!
interface GigabitEthernet0/1
no ip address
duplex auto
!
interface GigabitEthernet0/1.10
encapsulation dot1Q 10
ip address 192.168.10.1 255.255.255.0
!
interface GigabitEthernet0/1.20
encapsulation dot1Q 20
ip address 192.168.20.1 255.255.255.0
!
interface GigabitEthernet0/2
no ip address
duplex auto
speed auto
shutdown
!
end
```

Floor1Switch#show running-config
```
Building configuration...

Current configuration : 1244 bytes
!
hostname Floor1Switch
!
interface FastEthernet0/1
!
interface FastEthernet0/2
!
interface FastEthernet0/3
!
```

```
interface FastEthernet0/4
!
interface FastEthernet0/5
!
interface FastEthernet0/6
!
interface FastEthernet0/7
!
interface FastEthernet0/8
!
interface FastEthernet0/9
!
interface FastEthernet0/10
switchport access vlan 10
switchport mode access
!
interface FastEthernet0/11
!
interface FastEthernet0/12
!
interface FastEthernet0/13
!
interface FastEthernet0/14
!
interface FastEthernet0/15
!
interface FastEthernet0/16
!
interface FastEthernet0/17
!
interface FastEthernet0/18
!
interface FastEthernet0/19
!
interface FastEthernet0/20
switchport access vlan 20
switchport mode access
!
interface FastEthernet0/21
!
interface FastEthernet0/22
!
interface FastEthernet0/23
!
interface FastEthernet0/24
!
interface GigabitEthernet0/1
!
interface GigabitEthernet0/2
!
shutdown
!
end
```

EXERCISE #32 – Troubleshooting Switch and VLAN Configuration #5

Background Information: A company has set up a basic router-on-a-stick network to serve two VLANs, which have been set up as VLAN 10 and VLAN 20. They also have a file server connected to their network on its own subnetwork. The technician has been unable to get the router-on-a-stick configuration to work and asks you for assistance.

Task: Use the output from the troubleshooting commands provided to identify the configuration error.

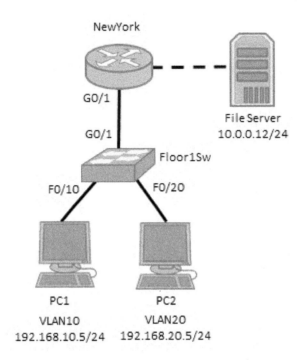

```
Floor1Switch#show interfaces trunk
Port        Mode          Encapsulation    Status      Native vlan
Gig0/1      on            802.1q           trunking    1

Port        Vlans allowed on trunk
Gig0/1

Port        Vlans allowed and active in management domain
Gig0/1      none

Port        Vlans in spanning tree forwarding state and not pruned
Gig0/1      none
```

EXERCISE #33 – Troubleshooting Switch and VLAN Configuration #6

Background Information: A new company has set up a basic router on a stick network to serve two VLANs, which have been set up as VLAN 10 and VLAN 20. They also have a file server connected to their network on its own subnetwork. The technician has been unable to get the router on a stick configuration to work and asks you for assistance.

Task: Use the output from the troubleshooting commands provided to identify the configuration error.

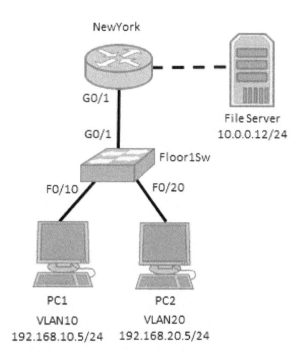

```
Command Prompt – PC1

C:\>ipconfig

IP Address......................: 192.168.10.5
Subnet Mask....................: 255.255.255.0
Default Gateway................: 192.168.10.1

C:\>ping 192.168.20.5

Pinging 192.168.20.5 with 32 bytes of data:

Request timed out.
Request timed out.
Request timed out.
Request timed out.
```

Floor1Switch#show vlan brief

```
VLAN Name                 Status     Ports
---- -------------------- ---------  -------------------------------
1    default              active     Fa0/1, Fa0/2, Fa0/3, Fa0/4
                                     Fa0/5, Fa0/6, Fa0/7, Fa0/8
                                     Fa0/9, Fa0/10, Fa0/12, Fa0/13
                                     Fa0/14, Fa0/15, Fa0/16, Fa0/17
                                     Fa0/18, Fa0/19, Fa0/21, Fa0/22
                                     Fa0/23, Fa0/24, Gig0/2
10   VLAN0010             active     Fa0/11
20   VLAN0020             active     Fa0/20
```

EXERCISE #34 – Troubleshooting Switch and VLAN Configuration #7

Background Information: A company has set up a network to support two floors of their New York office. The network needs to serve multiple VLANs, which thus far have been set up as VLAN 10 and VLAN 20. The technician has been unable to get the configuration to work for the user on the second floor and asks you for assistance.

Task: Use the output from the troubleshooting commands provided to identify the configuration error.

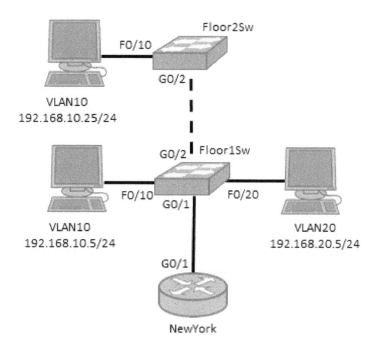

Floor1Sw#show vlan brief

VLAN	Name	Status	Ports
1	default	active	Fa0/1, Fa0/2, Fa0/3, Fa0/4
			Fa0/5, Fa0/6, Fa0/7, Fa0/8
			Fa0/9, Fa0/11, Fa0/12, Fa0/13
			Fa0/14, Fa0/15, Fa0/16, Fa0/17
			Fa0/18, Fa0/19, Fa0/21, Fa0/22
			Fa0/23, Fa0/24
10	VLAN0010	active	Fa0/10
20	VLAN0020	active	Fa0/20

Floor2Sw#show vlan brief

VLAN	Name	Status	Ports
1	default	active	Fa0/1, Fa0/2, Fa0/3, Fa0/4
			Fa0/5, Fa0/6, Fa0/7, Fa0/8
			Fa0/9, Fa0/11, Fa0/12, Fa0/13

```
                                         Fa0/14, Fa0/15, Fa0/16, Fa0/17
                                         Fa0/18, Fa0/19, Fa0/20, Fa0/21
                                         Fa0/22, Fa0/23, Fa0/24, Gig0/1
                                         Gig0/2
10      VLAN0010        active           Fa0/10
```

Floor2Sw#show interfaces g0/2 switchport
```
Name: Gig0/2
Switchport: Enabled
Administrative Mode: static access
Operational Mode: static access
Administrative Trunking Encapsulation: dot1q
Operational Trunking Encapsulation: native
Negotiation of Trunking: Off
Access Mode VLAN: 1 (default)
Trunking Native Mode VLAN: 1 (default)
Voice VLAN: none
```

EXERCISE #35 – Troubleshooting Switch and VLAN Configuration #8

Background Information: You have noticed that a company's topology documentation appears to be incorrect. Using the Cisco Discovery Protocol command output below, determine where the topology is incorrect.

Task: Use the output from the Cisco Discovery Protocol commands provided to identify the three topology documentation errors.

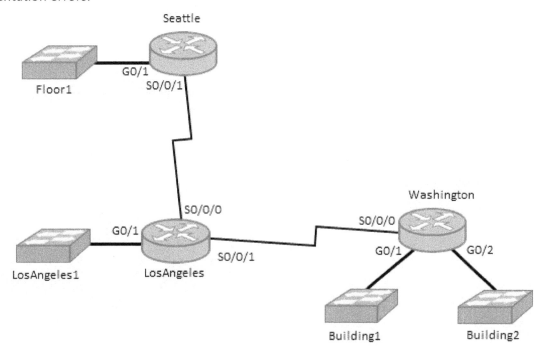

Washington#show cdp neighbors
```
Capability Codes: R - Router, T - Trans Bridge, B - Source Route Bridge,
S - Switch, H - Host, I - IGMP, r - Repeater, P - Phone
Device ID    Local Intrfce  Holdtme  Capability Platform  Port ID
LosAngeles   Ser 0/0/0        154       R          C2900     Ser 0/0/1
Seattle      Ser 0/0/1        149       R          C2900     Ser 0/0/0
Building1    Gig 0/1          175       S          2960      Gig 0/1
Building2    Gig 0/2          129       S          2960      Gig 0/2
```

Seattle#show cdp neighbors
```
Capability Codes: R - Router, T - Trans Bridge, B - Source Route Bridge,
S - Switch, H - Host, I - IGMP, r - Repeater, P - Phone
Device ID    Local Intrfce  Holdtme  Capability Platform  Port ID
Portland     Ser 0/1/0        111       R          C2900     Ser 0/1/0
Washington   Ser 0/0/0        133       R          C2900     Ser      0/0/1
LosAngeles   Ser 0/0/1        138       R          C2900     Ser 0/0/0
Floor1       Gig 0/1          115       S          2960      Gig 0/1
Floor2       Gig 0/2          120       S          2960      Gig 0/2
```

LosAngeles#show cdp neighbors
```
Capability Codes: R - Router, T - Trans Bridge, B - Source Route Bridge,
S - Switch, H - Host, I - IGMP, r - Repeater, P - Phone
Device ID    Local Intrfce   Holdtme  Capability  Platform  Port ID
Seattle      Ser 0/0/0       154      R           C2900     Ser 0/0/1
Washington   Ser 0/0/1       149      R           C2900     Ser 0/0/0
LosAngeles1  Gig 0/1         175      S           2960      Gig 0/1
```

EXERCISE #36 – Troubleshooting Switch and VLAN Configuration #9

Background Information: A network administrator has set up port security on her switches and has shutdown all unused ports. After setting up these security measures, the user at 192.168.10.5 has reported that he has been unable to reach the network after returning to the office on Monday morning.

Task: Use the output from the troubleshooting commands provided to identify the configuration error.

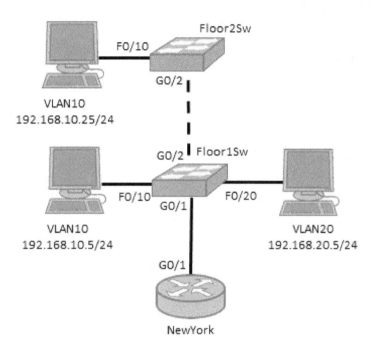

```
Floor1Sw#show running-config
Building configuration...

Current configuration : 1656 bytes
!
version 12.2
no service timestamps log datetime msec
no service timestamps debug datetime msec
no service password-encryption
!
hostname Floor1Sw
!
interface FastEthernet0/1
shutdown
!
interface FastEthernet0/2
shutdown
!
interface FastEthernet0/3
shutdown
!
interface FastEthernet0/4
```

```
shutdown
!
interface FastEthernet0/5
shutdown
!
interface FastEthernet0/6
shutdown
!
interface FastEthernet0/7
shutdown
!
interface FastEthernet0/8
shutdown
!
interface FastEthernet0/9
shutdown
!
interface FastEthernet0/10
switchport access vlan 10
switchport mode access
switchport port-security
switchport port-security mac-address sticky
switchport port-security mac-address sticky AACC.9729.38AC
!
interface FastEthernet0/11
shutdown
!
interface FastEthernet0/12
shutdown
!
interface FastEthernet0/13
shutdown
!
interface FastEthernet0/14
shutdown
!
interface FastEthernet0/15
shutdown
!
interface FastEthernet0/16
shutdown
!
interface FastEthernet0/17
shutdown
!
interface FastEthernet0/18
shutdown
!
interface FastEthernet0/19
shutdown
!
interface FastEthernet0/20
switchport access vlan 20
```

```
switchport mode access
switchport port-security
switchport port-security mac-address sticky
switchport port-security mac-address sticky AACC.97D8.4432
!
interface FastEthernet0/21
shutdown
!
interface FastEthernet0/22
shutdown
!
interface FastEthernet0/23
shutdown
!
interface FastEthernet0/24
shutdown
!
interface GigabitEthernet0/1
switchport trunk allowed vlan 1,10,20
switchport mode trunk
!
interface GigabitEthernet0/2
switchport trunk allowed vlan 1,10,20
switchport mode trunk
!
end
```

Floor1Sw#show port-security interface f0/10
```
Port Security : Enabled
Port Status : Secure-shutdown
Violation Mode : Shutdown
SecureStatic Address Aging : Disabled
Maximum MAC Addresses : 1
Total MAC Addresses : 1
Configured MAC Addresses : 0
Sticky MAC Addresses : 1
Last Source Address:Vlan : AACC.4138.6031:10
Security Violation Count : 1
```

Floor1Sw#show port-security int f0/20
```
Port Security : Enabled
Port Status : Secure-up
Violation Mode : Shutdown
SecureStatic Address Aging : Disabled
Maximum MAC Addresses : 1
Total MAC Addresses : 1
Configured MAC Addresses : 0
Sticky MAC Addresses : 1
Last Source Address:Vlan : ABBA.C91F.1809:20
Security Violation Count : 0
```

SOLUTIONS TO EXERCISES FOR CHAPTER 5

SOLUTION - EXERCISE #28

In this router-on-a-stick exercise, the command prompt from PC1 confirms that the host has an IP address and default gateway correctly configured for VLAN 10, but it is unable to ping the user on VLAN 20. The router's *show running-config* command output shows us the error. Notice on the sub-interface of G0/1.10 that the encapsulation is set for VLAN 12, not VLAN 10. The command *encapsulation dot1q* encapsulates traffic using IEEE 802.1Q for VLANs, and must include the specific VLAN ID as such: *encapsulation dot1q VLAN-ID*. This error would work if the VLAN was VLAN 12, but will not work for any other VLAN.

SOLUTION - EXERCISE #29

In this exercise, the command prompt from PC1 confirms that the host has an IP address and default gateway correctly configured for VLAN 10, but it is unable to ping the user on VLAN 20. The router is correctly configured; however, the switch's running configuration shows us the issue. In the *show running-config* output, switchport F0/10 is placed correctly into VLAN 10 but is set to a mode of trunk instead of access. Any switchport accessing a specific VLAN must be set as an access port. Keep in mind that access ports on a switch are designed to serve one host device operating on one VLAN, while trunk ports are specifically intended to transport multi-VLAN traffic.

SOLUTION - EXERCISE #30

This router-on-a-stick exercise has an added file server on its own LAN. Just as in the last exercise, the command prompt from PC1 confirms that the host has an IP address and default gateway correctly configured for VLAN 10, but it is unable to ping the user on the VLAN 20. The switch's *show vlan brief* command output is correct and as expected. The router's *show running-config* command output shows us the error, which is that the router has no sub-interface identified for VLAN10. We should see an additional interface listed on the router in this example – interface G0/1.10 with encapsulation dot1q 10.

SOLUTION - EXERCISE #31

In this exercise, we can locate the error in two locations. First, the switch's *show vlan brief* command output shows that interface G0/1 is currently in VLAN 1, which indicates that it is not set to trunk mode. We confirm this again in the switch's *show running-config* command output, where we can see that interface G0/1 is not set to trunk mode. If it were, the output line *switchport mode trunk* would be present.

SOLUTION - EXERCISE #32

In this exercise, the output from the *show interfaces trunk* reveals the error, which is that the switch interface g0/1 is a trunk but is not allowing any VLANs. If VLANs 10 and 20 were allowed on the trunk as needed, they would be listed in the output. To correct this issue, we would need to add the command *switchport trunk allowed vlan 10,20* to interface G0/1.

SOLUTION - EXERCISE #33

A careful look at the output from the *show vlan brief* command shows us that interface F0/11 has been assigned to VLAN 10, while interface F0/10 remains in VLAN 1. This will cause the host to not be able to reach the router, since the router assumedly does not have a sub-interface for VLAN 1.

SOLUTION - EXERCISE #34

We can find the error in this exercise on the Floor2Sw switch. Note from the *show interfaces G0/2 switchport* output, as well as the *show vlan brief* output, that interface G0/2 is not set to trunk mode (it is still set to static access). Since this port has not been set to trunk, it will not carry the VLAN tagged traffic of VLAN10. Note that Cisco switches in the Catalyst series using Dynamic Trunking Protocol automatically default to a trunk configuration of dynamic auto. Dynamic auto is a passive state that will not move the switch port to a setting of trunk unless the connecting device's port has a setting of dynamic desirable or trunk. If both devices have ports set to dynamic auto or access, the connection will not move to a trunking state.

SOLUTION - EXERCISE #35

In this exercise, we can review the output from the Cisco Discovery Protocol on various devices to locate the three topology documentation errors. They are 1) the Seattle and Washington routers are connected via a serial connection, 2) the Seattle router is connected to another router named Portland via its serial0/1/0 interface, and 3) the Seattle router is receiving CDP notifications from a second switch named Floor2, which is connected to its G0/2 interface. Here is the correct topology for comparison:

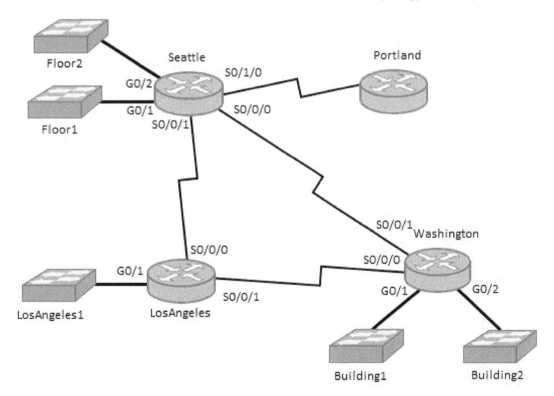

SOLUTION - EXERCISE #36

The running-config output on Floor1Sw confirms that all unused ports are in a shutdown state and that the access ports in use (F0/10 and F0/20) have sticky port-security applied and have received traffic from an initial MAC address. Upon viewing the *show port-security* command output for F0/10 and F0/20, we can see that F0/10 has been placed in a secure-shutdown state and its violation counter has been set at one, indicating a violation has occurred. In this example, the switch noticed a second MAC address (presumably the user who contacted the help desk), which was unauthorized due to the sticky MAC setting first documenting a different MAC address. This caused the port to move into a state of shutdown.

CHAPTER 6: Network Address Translation

Network address translation (NAT) is one of the more challenging topics within the CCENT exam content, but Cisco doesn't intend to ask highly detailed questions related to the topic. For the CCENT exam, you'll only need to be familiar with the following areas related to NAT:

> *4.7 Configure, verify, and troubleshoot inside source NAT*
> - *4.7.a Static*
> - *4.7.b Pool*
> - *4.7.c PAT*

Notice from this objective that you'll need be able to identify the differences between the three types of NAT: static, dynamic (pool) and port address translation (PAT), and troubleshoot each. You'll also need to understand the differences between inside, outside, global and local addresses. Regarding troubleshooting, you can expect to see questions that relate to the follow NAT issues:

1. The inside and outside interfaces for NAT are incorrectly defined.
2. The ACL that is bound to NAT is incorrect, or is incorrectly bound to NAT.
3. The NAT pool is not correctly defined.
4. The overload tag is not set to enable port address translation (PAT).

To troubleshoot these issues, there are three show and debug commands that you are expected to know and use related to NAT, in addition to the show commands used to view interfaces and access control lists, which can assist in verifying NAT configuration. The commands are:

debug ip nat

The *debug ip nat* command turns on debugging for NAT and enables you to verify that NAT is operating correctly. In a production environment, be sure to turn debugging off once it's no longer needed as it can become resource-intensive.

show ip nat statistics

The *show ip nat statistics* command is used to verify the interfaces that are translating NAT, and to verify that translations are occurring. This command will be one of the first commands to use to investigate and troubleshoot NAT.

show ip nat translations

The *show ip nat translations* command shows you any translations that are currently held in the NAT table, which is used to verify that NAT is functioning and to determine which addresses are translated.

EXERCISE #37 – Troubleshooting Network Address Translation #1

Background Information: An organization has set up a basic dynamic NAT environment, where host devices from the inside network of 192.168.10.0/24 are translated into addresses from the pool of 205.165.222.1 – 205.165.222.10. The translations are not working correctly.

Task: Use the output from the troubleshooting commands provided to identify the configuration error.

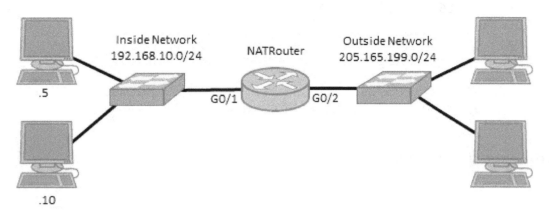

NATRouter#show ip nat statistics
```
Total translations: 0 (0 static, 0 dynamic, 0 extended)
Outside Interfaces: GigabitEthernet0/1
Inside Interfaces: GigabitEthernet0/2
Hits: 0 Misses: 0
Expired translations: 0
Dynamic mappings:
-- Inside Source
access-list 1 pool NATPool refCount 0
pool NATPool: netmask 255.255.255.0
start 205.165.222.1 end 205.165.222.10
```

NATRouter#show running-config
```
Building configuration...

Current configuration : 938 bytes
!
version 15.1
no service timestamps log datetime msec
no service timestamps debug datetime msec
no service password-encryption
!
hostname NATRouter
!
interface GigabitEthernet0/0
no ip address
duplex auto
speed auto
shutdown
```

```
!
interface GigabitEthernet0/1
ip address 192.168.10.1 255.255.255.0
ip nat outside
duplex auto
speed auto
!
interface GigabitEthernet0/2
ip address 205.165.199.1 255.255.255.0
ip nat inside
duplex auto
speed auto
!
ip nat pool NATPool 205.165.222.1 205.165.222.10 netmask 255.255.255.0
ip nat inside source list 1 pool NATPool
ip classless
!
ip flow-export version 9
!
!
access-list 1 permit host 192.168.10.5
access-list 1 permit host 192.168.10.10
!
end
```

EXERCISE #38 – Troubleshooting Network Address Translation #2

Background Information: An organization has set up a dynamic NAT environment with NAT overload, or PAT, where host devices from the inside network of 192.168.10.0/24 are translated into addresses from the pool of 205.165.222.1 – 205.165.222.10. The translations are not working correctly.

Task: Use the output from the troubleshooting commands provided to identify the configuration error.

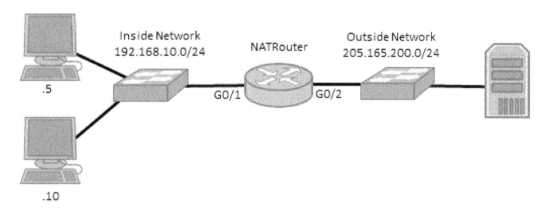

```
NATRouter#show ip nat translations
NATRouter#


NATRouter#show access-lists
Standard IP access list 1
      10 permit 172.16.100.0 0.0.0.255


NATRouter#show running-config
Building configuration...

Current configuration : 938 bytes
!
version 15.1
no service timestamps log datetime msec
no service timestamps debug datetime msec
no service password-encryption
!
hostname NATRouter
!
interface GigabitEthernet0/0
no ip address
duplex auto
speed auto
shutdown
!
interface GigabitEthernet0/1
ip address 192.168.10.1 255.255.255.0
ip nat inside
```

```
duplex auto
speed auto
!
interface GigabitEthernet0/2
ip address 205.165.200.1 255.255.255.0
ip nat outside
duplex auto
speed auto
!
ip nat pool NATPool 205.165.222.1 205.165.222.10 netmask 255.255.255.0
ip nat inside source list 1 pool NATPool overload
ip classless
!
ip flow-export version 9
!
!
access-list 1 permit 172.16.100.0 0.0.0.255
!
end
```

EXERCISE #39 – Troubleshooting Network Address Translation #3

Background Information: An organization has set up a dynamic NAT environment with NAT overload, or PAT, where a network of 50 host devices from the inside network of 192.168.10.0/24 are translated into addresses from the pool of 205.165.222.1 – 205.165.222.2. It appears that a few users can access resources out of the network, but others cannot.

Task: Use the output from the troubleshooting commands provided to identify the configuration error.

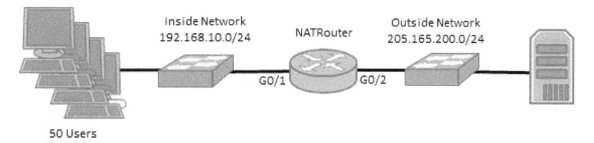

```
NATRouter#show running-config
Building configuration...

Current configuration : 938 bytes
!
version 15.1
no service timestamps log datetime msec
no service timestamps debug datetime msec
no service password-encryption
!
hostname NATRouter
!
interface GigabitEthernet0/0
no ip address
duplex auto
speed auto
shutdown
!
interface GigabitEthernet0/1
ip address 192.168.10.1 255.255.255.0
ip nat inside
duplex auto
speed auto
!
interface GigabitEthernet0/2
ip address 205.165.200.1 255.255.255.0
ip nat outside
duplex auto
speed auto
!
ip nat pool NATPool 205.165.222.1 205.165.222.2 netmask 255.255.255.0
ip nat inside source list 1 pool NATPool
ip classless
```

```
!
ip flow-export version 9
!
access-list 1 permit 192.168.10.0 0.0.0.255
!
end
```

```
ip flow-export version 9
access-list 1 permit 192.168.10.0 0.0.0.255
```

EXERCISE #40 – Troubleshooting Network Address Translation #4

Background Information: An organization has set up a dynamic NAT environment with NAT overload, or PAT, where a network of 50 host devices from the inside network of 192.168.10.0/24 are translated into addresses from the pool of 205.165.222.1 – 205.165.222.2. The port address translations are not working correctly.

Task: Use the output from the troubleshooting commands provided to identify the configuration error.

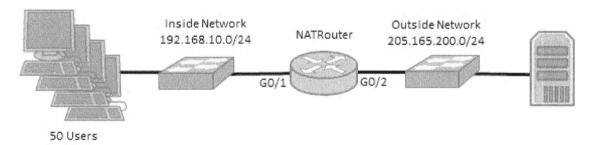

```
NATRouter#show access-lists
Standard IP access list 1
      10 permit 192.168.10.0 0.0.0.255


NATRouter#show running-config
Building configuration...

Current configuration : 938 bytes
!
version 15.1
no service timestamps log datetime msec
no service timestamps debug datetime msec
no service password-encryption
!
hostname NATRouter
!
interface GigabitEthernet0/0
no ip address
duplex auto
speed auto
shutdown
!
interface GigabitEthernet0/1
ip address 192.168.10.1 255.255.255.0
ip nat inside
duplex auto
speed auto
!
interface GigabitEthernet0/2
ip address 205.165.200.1 255.255.255.0
ip nat outside
```

```
duplex auto
speed auto
!
ip nat pool NATPool 205.165.222.1 205.165.222.2 netmask 255.255.255.0
ip nat inside source list 25 pool NATPool overload
ip classless
!
ip flow-export version 9
!
!
access-list 1 permit 192.168.10.0 0.0.0.255
!
end
```

EXERCISE #41 – Troubleshooting Network Address Translation #5

Background Information: An organization has set up a static NAT environment for its user on PC1, however the translation is not working correctly.

Task: Use the output from the troubleshooting commands provided to identify the configuration error.

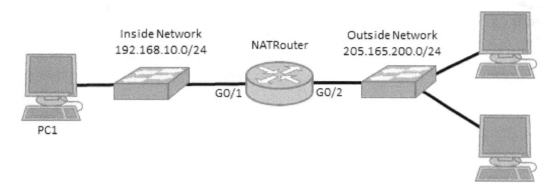

```
Command Prompt – PC1

C:\>ipconfig

IP Address........................: 192.168.10.5
Subnet Mask.....................: 255.255.255.0
Default Gateway.................: 192.168.10.1
```

```
NATRouter#show running-config
Building configuration...

Current configuration : 994 bytes
!
version 15.1
no service timestamps log datetime msec
no service timestamps debug datetime msec
no service password-encryption
!
hostname NATRouter
!
interface GigabitEthernet0/0
no ip address
duplex auto
speed auto
shutdown
!
interface GigabitEthernet0/1
ip address 192.168.10.1 255.255.255.0
ip nat inside
duplex auto
speed auto
```

```
!
interface GigabitEthernet0/2
ip address 205.165.200.1 255.255.255.0
ip nat outside
duplex auto
speed auto
!
interface Vlan1
no ip address
shutdown
!
ip nat inside source static 192.168.10.2 205.165.222.5
!
end
```

EXERCISE #42 – Troubleshooting Network Address Translation #6

Background Information: An organization has set up a static NAT environment for its user on PC1, but the translation is not working correctly.

Task: Use the output from the troubleshooting commands provided to identify the configuration error.

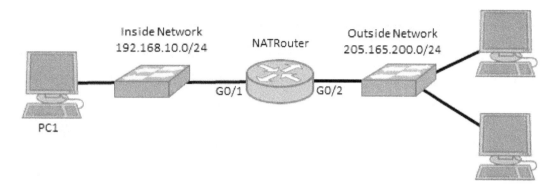

```
NATRouter#show running-config
Building configuration...

Current configuration : 994 bytes
!
version 15.1
no service timestamps log datetime msec
no service timestamps debug datetime msec
no service password-encryption
!
hostname NATRouter
!
interface GigabitEthernet0/0
no ip address
duplex auto
speed auto
shutdown
!
interface GigabitEthernet0/1
ip address 192.168.10.1 255.255.255.0
duplex auto
speed auto
!
```

```
interface GigabitEthernet0/2
ip address 205.165.200.1 255.255.255.0
duplex auto
speed auto
!
interface Vlan1
no ip address
shutdown
!
ip nat inside source static 192.168.10.5 205.165.222.5
!
end
```

SOLUTIONS TO EXERCISES FOR CHAPTER 6

SOLUTION - EXERCISE #37

This is a dynamic (pool) NAT exercise with a common issue, which is that the interfaces are labeled inside out, or backwards. A look at the *show ip nat statistics* command shows that the inside and outside interfaces are opposite of the topology, and the *show running-config* confirms that as well. The other components of the configuration are correct, so if an administrator were to swap the *ip nat inside* and *ip nat outside* configurations, the NAT set-up would function correctly.

SOLUTION - EXERCISE #38

This is another NAT exercise with a common issue. We see that the *show ip nat translations* command has not recorded any translations (since it returned no output) and the *show access-lists* command shows one standard ACL that permits the 172.16.100.0 network only. This network, of course, is not the network that is the target for translation (we are translating the 192.168.10.0 network), and therefore the ACL ends up denying the network that needs to be permitted. The *show running-config* confirms this as well, and additionally confirms that the ACL is bound to NAT, and that the interfaces are configured for NAT translation. To correct this issue, the network administrator should adjust the ACL to specifically permit the correct network, or bind a new ACL to NAT.

SOLUTION - EXERCISE #39

This is a challenging exercise because the error is so small that it can easily go unnoticed. This is an example where an administrator intended to configure port address translation, but the configuration is dynamic NAT, not PAT. The difference is in the *ip nat inside source list 1 pool NATPool* line in the *show running-config* command. This line should have the additional word *overload* at the end of the configuration line, which would indicate that port address translation is enabled. When port address translation is enabled, all hosts will be able to simultaneously share the two NAT addresses by utilizing unique ephemeral port numbers, which will be appended to the IP address being used in the pool.

SOLUTION - EXERCISE #40

In this PAT example, the standard access list is not correctly bound to the NAT pool. Note in the binding line *ip nat inside source list 25 pool NATPool overload* that the line is binding standard ACL 25, not ACL 1. Our *show access-lists* command output shows that there is no ACL 25 (only an ACL 1), and the output from the *show running-config* confirms that. While the NAT configuration is set up correctly (and functioning as PAT), it is bound to a non-existent ACL. This causes the router to be unable to identify which addresses are the target of translation.

SOLUTION - EXERCISE #41

This is a basic static NAT exercise with another common error. Note that the IP address of PC1 is confirmed as 192.168.10.5 in the command prompt output, however the static NAT command is set to translate a different IP address – 192.168.10.2. This configuration means that there is no NAT setting for this user. The IP addresses must be made to match, either on the router or on the host.

SOLUTION - EXERCISE #42

In this static NAT exercise, the static NAT command is correct in the *show running-config* output, but the interfaces G0/1 and G0/2 are not marked as inside or outside. They need to have *the ip nat inside* and *ip nat outside* commands applied, as appropriate.

CHAPTER 7: Device Management and Security

Cisco requires that CCENT exam takers be able to troubleshoot basic device hardening concepts and use troubleshooting tools such as extended ping, extended traceroute, logging and terminal monitor. Specifically, the exam objectives are:

> *5.4 Configure, verify, and troubleshoot basic device hardening*
> - *5.4.a Local authentication*
> - *5.4.b Secure password*
> - *5.4.c Access to device*
>   - *5.4.c. [i] Source address*
>   - *5.4.c. [ii] Telnet/SSH*
> - *5.4.d Login banner*
>
> *5.6 Use Cisco IOS tools to troubleshoot and resolve problems*
> - *5.6.a Ping and traceroute with extended option*
> - *5.6.b Terminal monitor*
> - *5.6.c Log events*

There are several commands that can assist us with troubleshooting device management and security, with the *show running-config* command certainly being the most useful. Other relevant commands include:

extended ping / extended traceroute

Extended ping is just a variation of the ping command and is most helpful for troubleshooting when we want to specify a different source address of the ping. While a standard ping is sourced from the router interface that it exits, the extended ping can be sourced from any other interface on that router, thereby allowing for a more in-depth analysis of reachability, since you can now ping from a different interface and network and in effect ping across the router. The extended ping also allows for consistent or sustained pinging, which is useful for observing problems in reachability while changes to the network are being completed. To issue an extended ping in the IOS, simply enter the ping command without specifying a destination address. The prompts that follow will enable you to dictate the characteristics of the ping that will be sent. Extended traceroute is like the extended ping in that you can also specify a different source address that the traceroute originates from. To issue an extended traceroute, enter the traceroute command without a destination address.

show ssh

This command shows the Secure Shell (SSH) connections to a device. The *show ssh* command is very useful when we not only want to verify current SSH connections to the device, but also the username that is connecting.

show ip ssh

The *show ip ssh* command displays Secure Shell (SSH) version and configuration information for the device. It will also provide important information regarding connection timeouts.

show logging

The *show logging* command is useful for providing information about the logging service on the device. This includes logging statistics and the logging configuration. Additionally, we can use the show logging command to view the logging messages that are in the buffer, which is helpful in troubleshooting recent issues that may have been logged.

EXERCISE #43 – Troubleshooting Device Management and Security #1

Background Information: A colleague attempted to configure basic device hardening on the three routers of the network, including establishing login banners and secure passwords.

Task: Verify that all three routers have a) appropriate motd banners, b) passwords for the enable prompt and console and VTY connections, and c) encrypted service, console, VTY and enable passwords. Document any instances where these requirements have not been met on the routers.

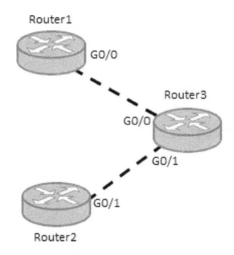

```
Router1(config)#do show running-config
Building configuration...

Current configuration : 906 bytes
!
version 15.1
no service timestamps log datetime msec
no service timestamps debug datetime msec
service password-encryption
!
hostname Router1
!
enable password 7 0822455D0A16
!
interface GigabitEthernet0/0
ip address 172.16.1.1 255.255.255.252
duplex auto
speed auto
!
interface GigabitEthernet0/1
no ip address
duplex auto
speed auto
shutdown
!
```

```
banner motd # This is a secure network system. No unauthorized access
permitted. #
!
line con 0
password 7 08224F4B070D
login
!
line vty 0 4
password 7 08224F4B070D
login
line vty 5 15
password 7 08224F4B070D
login
!
end
```

Router2#show running-config
```
Building configuration...

Current configuration : 824 bytes
!
version 15.1
no service timestamps log datetime msec
no service timestamps debug datetime msec
no service password-encryption
!
hostname Router2
!
interface GigabitEthernet0/0
no ip address
duplex auto
speed auto
shutdown
!
interface GigabitEthernet0/1
ip address 172.16.2.1 255.255.255.252
duplex auto
speed auto
!
line con 0
!
line vty 0 4
login
!
end
```

Router3#show running-config
```
Building configuration...

Current configuration : 824 bytes
!
```

```
version 15.1
no service timestamps log datetime msec
no service timestamps debug datetime msec
no service password-encryption
!
hostname Router3
!
enable password cisco
!
interface GigabitEthernet0/0
ip address 172.16.1.2 255.255.255.252
duplex auto
speed auto
!
interface GigabitEthernet0/1
ip address 172.16.2.2 255.255.255.252
duplex auto
speed auto
!
banner motd # This is a secure network system. No unauthorized access
permitted. #
!
line con 0
!
line vty 0 4
login
!
end
```

EXERCISE #44 – Troubleshooting Device Management and Security #2

<u>Background Information</u>: You oversee a four-router network. You want to verify that SSH version 2 is configured correctly on all four of the routers. Additionally, you want to verify that no one can access the routers via SSH except for your two administrators, Dave and Linda.

<u>Task</u>: Use the output from the troubleshooting commands provided to verify that SSH is configured correctly on all routers and that only Dave and Linda have access to the routers via SSH. Document anywhere in the command outputs provided that these configurations are not correct.

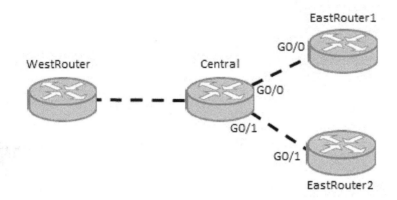

```
WestRouter#show ip ssh
SSH Enabled - version 2.0
Authentication timeout: 120 secs; Authentication retries: 3


Central#show ip ssh
SSH Enabled - version 2.0
Authentication timeout: 120 secs; Authentication retries: 3


EastRouter1#show ip ssh
SSH Disabled - version 1.99
%Please create RSA keys (of atleast 768 bits size) to enable SSH v2.
Authentication timeout: 120 secs; Authentication retries: 3


EastRouter2#show running-config
Building configuration...

Current configuration : 982 bytes
!
version 15.1
no service timestamps log datetime msec
no service timestamps debug datetime msec
service password-encryption
!
hostname EastRouter2
!
```

```
enable secret 5 $1$mERr$hx5rVt7rPNoS4wqbXKX7m0
!
ip cef
no ipv6 cef
!
username Dave secret 5 $1$mERr$hx5rVt7rPNoS4wqbXKX7m0
username Linda secret 5 S4wqbXKX7m0$1$mERr$hx5rVt7rPNs
!
ip ssh version 2
ip domain-name s1.yourcompany.com
!
interface GigabitEthernet0/0
no ip address
duplex auto
speed auto
shutdown
!
interface GigabitEthernet0/1
ip address 10.0.0.1 255.255.255.252
duplex auto
speed auto
!
line con 0
!
line vty 0 4
login local
transport input ssh
line vty 5 15
login local
transport input ssh
!
end
```

WestRouter#show ssh
```
%No SSHv2 server connections running.
%No SSHv1 server connections running.
```

Central#show ssh
```
Connection Ver   Mode  Encryption State           Username
389         1.99 IN    aes128-cbc Session Started Steven
389         1.99 OUT   aes128-cbc Session Started Steven
%No SSHv1 server connections running.
```

EastRouter1#show ssh
```
%No SSHv2 server connections running.
%No SSHv1 server connections running.
```

```
EastRouter2#show ssh
Connection Ver    Mode  Encryption State            Username
389            1.99 IN    aes128-cbc Session Started Dave
389            1.99 OUT   aes128-cbc Session Started Dave
%No SSHv1 server connections running.
```

```
EastRouter2#show ssh
Connection Ver    Mode  Encryption State            Username
```

EXERCISE #45 – Troubleshooting Device Management and Security #3

Background Information: You want to verify that logging is enabled and is being logged to both the console and the internal buffer on all three of your routers. You run the *show logging* command on each router to determine if these settings are enabled.

Task: Use the output from the troubleshooting commands provided to verify that all three of your routers are logging to the console and to the internal buffer. Document any instances where that is not the case.

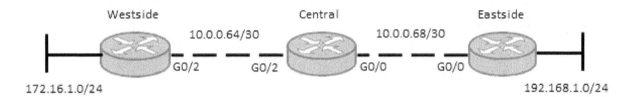

```
Westside#show logging
Syslog logging: enabled (0 messages dropped, 0 messages rate-limited,
0 flushes, 0 overruns, xml disabled, filtering disabled)

No Active Message Discriminator.

No Inactive Message Discriminator.

Console logging: disabled
Monitor logging: level debugging, 9 messages logged, xml disabled,
filtering disabled
Buffer logging: level debugging, 0 messages logged, xml disabled,
filtering disabled

Logging Exception size (4096 bytes)
Count and timestamp logging messages: disabled
Persistent logging: disabled

No active filter modules.

ESM: 0 messages dropped
Trap logging: level informational, 10 message lines logged
Log Buffer (4096 bytes):


Central#show logging
Syslog logging: enabled (0 messages dropped, 0 messages rate-limited,
0 flushes, 0 overruns, xml disabled, filtering disabled)

No Active Message Discriminator.

No Inactive Message Discriminator.

Console logging: level debugging, 14 messages logged, xml disabled,
```

filtering disabled
Monitor logging: level debugging, 14 messages logged, xml disabled,
filtering disabled
Buffer logging: level debugging, 0 messages logged, xml disabled,
filtering disabled

Logging Exception size (4096 bytes)
Count and timestamp logging messages: disabled
Persistent logging: disabled

No active filter modules.

ESM: 0 messages dropped
Trap logging: level informational, 10 message lines logged
Log Buffer (4096 bytes):

Eastside#show logging
Syslog logging: enabled (0 messages dropped, 0 messages rate-limited,
0 flushes, 0 overruns, xml disabled, filtering disabled)

No Active Message Discriminator.

No Inactive Message Discriminator.

Console logging: level debugging, 7 messages logged, xml disabled,
filtering disabled
Monitor logging: level debugging, 7 messages logged, xml disabled,
filtering disabled
Buffer logging: disabled, xml disabled,filtering disabled

Logging Exception size (4096 bytes)
Count and timestamp logging messages: disabled
Persistent logging: disabled

No active filter modules.

ESM: 0 messages dropped
Trap logging: level informational, 10 message lines logged
Log Buffer (4096 bytes):

SOLUTIONS TO EXERCISES FOR CHAPTER 7

SOLUTION - EXERCISE #43

In this exercise, Router1 is correctly secured with a motd banner and service password-encryption, and has passwords assigned to the console and VTY lines. Router2 does not have any of the correct configurations, including having no passwords or banner, and no service password-encryption enabled. Router3 does have a banner and an enable password, but that password is not encrypted and is in cleartext. Router3 also does not have the console or VTY lines secured with a password and does not have any passwords encrypted with the service password-encryption feature.

SOLUTION - EXERCISE #44

In this exercise, there are two configuration errors that need to be corrected, based on the outputs provided. First, EastRouter1 is not configured for SSH based on its *show ip ssh* command output. From the output of the other commands, we can verify that SSH is configured on the other three routers. Secondly, we can see from the *show ssh* command output on the Central router that there is a user named Steven who is logged into that router. We have been told that no usernames other than Dave and Linda should be allowed to access the devices. From the command outputs provided, we are not able to fully identify all usernames that may have SSH access on all four routers. The full configuration for SSH consists of configuring the domain name with the *ip domain-name* command, generating the RSA key pairs with the *crypto key generate rsa* command, setting the SSH version to version 2 with the *ip ssh version 2* command, and adding appropriate usernames with the *username* command. Also required is to ensure the VTY lines will allow SSH connectivity by entering the *transport input ssh* command into the vty line configuration prompt.

SOLUTION - EXERCISE #45

From the *show logging* command outputs, we can see that syslog logging is enabled on all devices, but logging to the console is disabled on the Westside router, and logging to the internal buffer is disabled on the Eastside router. The central router has logging configured correctly.

CHAPTER 8: Comprehensive Exercises

The comprehensive exercises in this section pull from the prior sections in this book and are designed to help you learn to troubleshoot open-ended problems. This means that these exercises could focus on any component of a configuration, no matter how large or small, and may include anywhere from one to three errors. Some of these exercises will be rather challenging, while others may be deceptively simple (just like in a live environment.) Before beginning these exercises, make sure you're comfortable with troubleshooting all the previously covered topics, including NAT, DHCP, ACLs, switchport security, interface configurations and RIP. Your ability to troubleshoot these exercises successfully, with a solid understanding of the underlying concepts, is a good indication of mastery of the troubleshooting content on the CCENT exam. Good luck!

EXERCISE #46 – Comprehensive Exercise #1

Background Information: Your company, S&L Bank, has acquired a competing bank, and after interviewing their regional branch managers, you have learned that there have been several issues with their network. Specifically, the Los Angeles branch sales team computers have APIPA addresses, the users in the Miami branch have several computers that will not connect to the network, and the File Server is having network connectivity issues.

Task: Use the output from the troubleshooting commands provided to identify the three configuration errors.

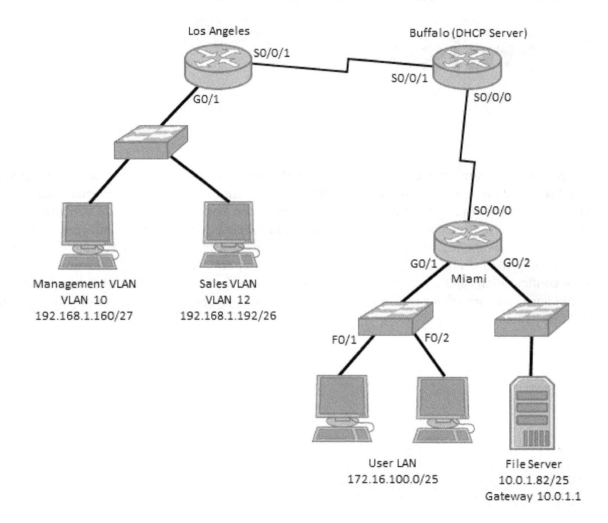

Los Angeles

Buffalo (DHCP Server)

Management VLAN
VLAN 10
192.168.1.160/27

Sales VLAN
VLAN 12
192.168.1.192/26

Miami

User LAN
172.16.100.0/25

File Server
10.0.1.82/25
Gateway 10.0.1.1

Command Prompt – File Server
C:\>ipconfig
IP Address.........................: 10.0.1.82
Subnet Mask.....................: 255.255.255.128
Default Gateway................: 10.0.1.1

LosAngelesSwitch#show vlan brief

```
VLAN Name                 Status    Ports
---- -------------------- --------- -------------------------------
1    default              active    Fa0/1, Fa0/2, Fa0/3, Fa0/4
                                    Fa0/5, Fa0/6, Fa0/7, Fa0/8
                                    Fa0/9, Fa0/11, Fa0/13, Fa0/14
                                    Fa0/15, Fa0/16, Fa0/17, Fa0/18
                                    Fa0/19, Fa0/20, Fa0/21, Fa0/22
                                    Fa0/23, Fa0/24, Gig0/2
10   VLAN0010             active    Fa0/10
12   VLAN0012             active    Fa0/12
```

LosAngeles#show running-config
```
Building configuration...

Current configuration : 1171 bytes
!
version 15.1
no service timestamps log datetime msec
no service timestamps debug datetime msec
no service password-encryption
!
hostname LosAngeles
!
interface GigabitEthernet0/0
no ip address
duplex auto
speed auto
shutdown
!
interface GigabitEthernet0/1
no ip address
duplex auto
speed auto
!
interface GigabitEthernet0/1.10
encapsulation dot1Q 10
ip address 192.168.1.161 255.255.255.224
ip helper-address 10.0.0.2
!
interface GigabitEthernet0/1.12
encapsulation dot1Q 12
ip address 192.168.1.193 255.255.255.192
!
interface GigabitEthernet0/2
no ip address
duplex auto
speed auto
shutdown
!
interface Serial0/0/0
```

```
no ip address
shutdown
!
interface Serial0/0/1
ip address 10.0.0.1 255.255.255.252
clock rate 64000
!
router rip
version 2
network 10.0.0.0
network 192.168.1.0
no auto-summary
!
end
```

Buffalo#show running-config
```
Building configuration...

Current configuration : 1136 bytes
!
version 15.1
no service timestamps log datetime msec
no service timestamps debug datetime msec
no service password-encryption
!
hostname Buffalo
!
ip dhcp pool Mgmt
network 192.168.1.160 255.255.255.224
default-router 192.168.1.161
ip dhcp pool Sales
network 192.168.1.192 255.255.255.192
default-router 192.168.1.193
ip dhcp pool UserLAN
network 172.16.100.0 255.255.255.128
default-router 172.16.100.1
!
interface GigabitEthernet0/0
no ip address
duplex auto
speed auto
shutdown
!
interface GigabitEthernet0/1
no ip address
duplex auto
speed auto
shutdown
!
interface GigabitEthernet0/2
no ip address
duplex auto
```

```
speed auto
shutdown
!
interface Serial0/0/0
ip address 10.0.0.5 255.255.255.252
!
interface Serial0/0/1
ip address 10.0.0.2 255.255.255.252
!
interface Vlan1
no ip address
shutdown
!
router rip
version 2
network 10.0.0.0
no auto-summary
!
end
```

Miami#show running-config
```
Building configuration...

Current configuration : 1037 bytes
!
version 15.1
no service timestamps log datetime msec
no service timestamps debug datetime msec
no service password-encryption
!
hostname Miami
!
interface GigabitEthernet0/0
no ip address
duplex auto
speed auto
shutdown
!
interface GigabitEthernet0/1
ip address 172.16.100.1 255.255.255.128
ip helper-address 10.0.0.5
ip access-group 99 in
duplex auto
speed auto
!
interface GigabitEthernet0/2
ip address 10.0.1.1 255.255.255.252
duplex auto
speed auto
!
interface Serial0/0/0
ip address 10.0.0.6 255.255.255.252
```

```
clock rate 2000000
!
interface Serial0/0/1
no ip address
clock rate 2000000
shutdown
!
interface Vlan1
no ip address
shutdown
!
router rip
version 2
network 10.0.0.0
network 172.16.0.0
no auto-summary
!
access-list 99 deny host 192.168.1.162
!
end
```

EXERCISE #47 – Comprehensive Exercise #2

Background Information: Users on the 192.168.1.0/24 network are unable to connect to the 172.16.1.0/24 network.

Task: Use the output from the troubleshooting commands provided to identify the configuration error.

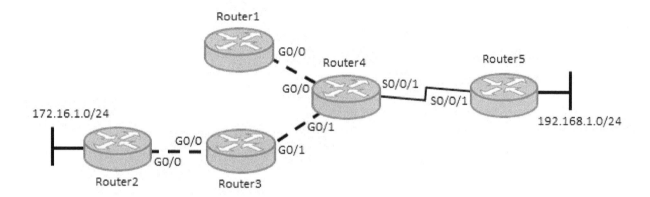

```
Router5#show ip route

Gateway of last resort is not set

10.0.0.0/8 is variably subnetted, 5 subnets, 2 masks
R     10.0.1.0/30 [120/2] via 10.0.4.1, 00:00:20, Serial0/0/1
R     10.0.2.0/30 [120/1] via 10.0.4.1, 00:00:20, Serial0/0/1
R     10.0.3.0/30 [120/1] via 10.0.4.1, 00:00:20, Serial0/0/1
C     10.0.4.0/30 is directly connected, Serial0/0/1
L     10.0.4.2/32 is directly connected, Serial0/0/1
192.168.1.0/24 is variably subnetted, 2 subnets, 2 masks
C     192.168.1.0/24 is directly connected, GigabitEthernet0/1
L     192.168.1.1/32 is directly connected, GigabitEthernet0/1


Router2#show protocols
Global values:
     Internet Protocol routing is enabled
GigabitEthernet0/0 is up, line protocol is up
     Internet address is 10.0.1.1/30
GigabitEthernet0/1 is up, line protocol is up
     Internet address is 172.16.1.1/24


Router2#show ip protocols
Routing Protocol is "rip"
Sending updates every 30 seconds, next due in 0 seconds
Invalid after 180 seconds, hold down 180, flushed after 240
Default version control: send version 2, receive 2
Automatic network summarization is not in effect
Maximum path: 4
```

```
Routing for Networks:
      10.0.0.0
Passive Interface(s):
Routing Information Sources:
      Gateway     Distance    Last Update
      10.0.1.2    120         00:00:24
Distance: (default is 120)
```

Router2#show running-config
```
Building configuration...

Current configuration : 772 bytes
!
version 15.1
no service timestamps log datetime msec
no service timestamps debug datetime msec
no service password-encryption
!
hostname Router2
!
interface GigabitEthernet0/0
ip address 10.0.1.1 255.255.255.252
duplex auto
speed auto
!
interface GigabitEthernet0/1
ip address 172.16.1.1 255.255.255.0
duplex auto
speed auto
!
interface GigabitEthernet0/2
no ip address
duplex auto
speed auto
shutdown
!
router rip
version 2
network 10.0.0.0
no auto-summary
!
end
```

EXERCISE #48 – Comprehensive Exercise #3

Background Information: The user on the 192.168.1.0/24 network cannot reach the user on the 192.168.2.0/24 network.

Task: Use the output from the troubleshooting commands provided to identify the configuration error.

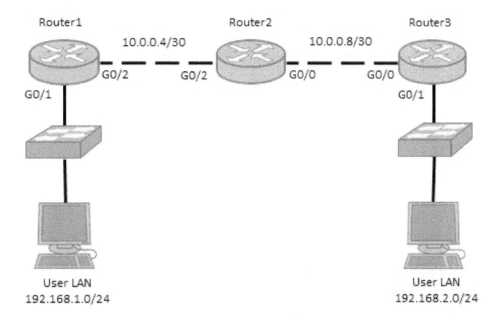

```
Router1#show running-config
Building configuration...

Current configuration : 802 bytes
!
version 15.1
no service timestamps log datetime msec
no service timestamps debug datetime msec
no service password-encryption
!
hostname Router1
!
spanning-tree mode pvst
!
interface GigabitEthernet0/0
no ip address
duplex auto
speed auto
shutdown
!
interface GigabitEthernet0/1
ip address 192.168.1.1 255.255.255.0
duplex auto
speed auto
!
```

```
interface GigabitEthernet0/2
ip address 10.0.0.5 255.255.255.252
duplex auto
speed auto
!
interface Vlan1
no ip address
shutdown
!
ip classless
ip route 0.0.0.0 0.0.0.0 GigabitEthernet0/2
!
ip flow-export version 9
!
end
```

Router2(config)#do show running-config
```
Building configuration...

Current configuration : 823 bytes
!
version 15.1
no service timestamps log datetime msec
no service timestamps debug datetime msec
no service password-encryption
!
hostname Router2
!
ip cef
no ipv6 cef
!
interface GigabitEthernet0/0
ip address 10.0.0.6 255.255.255.252
duplex auto
speed auto
!
interface GigabitEthernet0/1
no ip address
duplex auto
speed auto
shutdown
!
interface GigabitEthernet0/2
ip address 10.0.0.9 255.255.255.252
duplex auto
speed auto
!
interface Vlan1
no ip address
shutdown
!
ip classless
```

```
ip route 192.168.1.0 255.255.255.0 GigabitEthernet0/2
ip route 192.168.2.0 255.255.255.0 GigabitEthernet0/0
!
end
```

Router2#show ip interface brief

```
Interface            IP-Address OK? Status                Protocol
GigabitEthernet0/0   10.0.0.6   YES up                    up
GigabitEthernet0/1   unassigned YES administratively down down
GigabitEthernet0/2   10.0.0.9   YES up                    up
Vlan1                unassigned YES administratively down down
```

EXERCISE #49 – Comprehensive Exercise #4

Background Information: You are administering a two-location corporate WAN network that is configured with multiple VLANs. Users on VLAN 10 and VLAN 11 are reporting that they cannot reach the server on VLAN 13, even though they should be able to do so. You have not been able to verify that the user on VLAN 12 can connect to the server.

Task: Use the output from the troubleshooting commands provided to identify the two configuration errors.

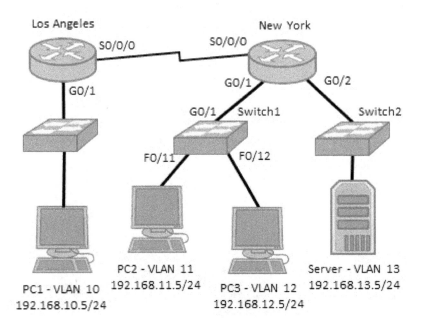

```
Switch1#show vlan brief

VLAN Name         Status        Ports
---- ---------    ---------     --------------------------------
1    default      active        Fa0/1, Fa0/2, Fa0/3, Fa0/4
                                Fa0/5, Fa0/6, Fa0/7, Fa0/8
                                Fa0/9, Fa0/10, Fa0/13, Fa0/14
                                Fa0/15, Fa0/16, Fa0/17, Fa0/18
                                Fa0/19, Fa0/20, Fa0/21, Fa0/22
                                Fa0/23, Fa0/24, Gig0/2
11   VLAN0011     active        Fa0/11
12   VLAN0012     active        Fa0/12
1002 fddi-default active
1003 token-ring-default active
1004 fddinet-default active
1005 trnet-default active
```

```
Command Prompt – PC1

C:\>ipconfig

IP Address.........................: 192.168.10.5
Subnet Mask.....................: 255.255.255.0
Default Gateway................: 192.168.10.1

C:\>ping 192.168.13.5

Pinging 192.168.13.5 with 32 bytes of data:

Request timed out.
Request timed out.
Request timed out.
Request timed out.
```

Switch1#show interfaces trunk
```
Port       Mode Encapsulation    Status      Native vlan
Gig0/1     on   802.1q           trunking    1

Port       Vlans allowed on trunk
Gig0/1     12

Port       Vlans allowed and active in management domain
Gig0/1     12

Port       Vlans in spanning tree forwarding state and not pruned
Gig0/1     12
```

```
Command Prompt – PC2

C:\>ipconfig

IP Address.........................: 192.168.11.5
Subnet Mask.....................: 255.255.255.0
Default Gateway................: 192.168.11.1

C:\>ping 192.168.13.5

Pinging 192.168.13.5 with 32 bytes of data:

Request timed out.
Request timed out.
Request timed out.
Request timed out.
```

Command Prompt – Server
C:\>ipconfig IP Address.......................: 192.168.133.5 Subnet Mask.....................: 255.255.255.0 Default Gateway.................: 192.168.13.1

EXERCISE #50 – Comprehensive Exercise #5

Background Information: Users on the 192.168.1.0/24 network are reporting that they cannot connect to the server on the 172.16.1.0/24 network. You are aware that your new network technician was working in all four routers on your network last night, but he is not in the office for you to confirm what configuration changes he may have made.

Task: Use the output from the troubleshooting commands provided to identify the configuration error.

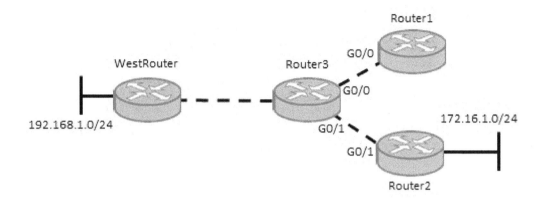

```
WestRouter#show ip protocols
Routing Protocol is "rip"
Sending updates every 30 seconds, next due in 8 seconds
Invalid after 180 seconds, hold down 180, flushed after 240
Outgoing update filter list for all interfaces is not set
Incoming update filter list for all interfaces is not set
Automatic network summarization is not in effect
Maximum path: 4
Routing for Networks:
     10.0.0.0
     192.168.1.0
Passive Interface(s):
Routing Information Sources:
     Gateway     Distance    Last Update
     10.10.1.1   120         00:00:02
Distance: (default is 120)
```

```
Router2#show ip route

Gateway of last resort is not set

10.0.0.0/8 is variably subnetted, 4 subnets, 2 masks
R      10.10.1.0/30 [120/1] via 10.10.3.1, 00:00:10, GigabitEthernet0/1
R      10.10.2.0/30 [120/1] via 10.10.3.1, 00:00:10, GigabitEthernet0/1
C      10.10.3.0/30 is directly connected, GigabitEthernet0/1
L      10.10.3.2/32 is directly connected, GigabitEthernet0/1
172.16.0.0/16 is variably subnetted, 2 subnets, 2 masks
C      172.16.1.0/24 is directly connected, GigabitEthernet0/2
```

```
L       172.16.1.1/32 is directly connected, GigabitEthernet0/2
R       192.168.1.0/24 [120/2] via 10.10.3.1, 00:00:10, GigabitEthernet0/1
```

Router3#show ip route

```
Gateway of last resort is 0.0.0.0 to network 0.0.0.0

        10.0.0.0/8 is variably subnetted, 6 subnets, 2 masks
C          10.10.1.0/30 is directly connected, GigabitEthernet0/2
L          10.10.1.1/32 is directly connected, GigabitEthernet0/2
C          10.10.2.0/30 is directly connected, GigabitEthernet0/0
L          10.10.2.1/32 is directly connected, GigabitEthernet0/0
C          10.10.3.0/30 is directly connected, GigabitEthernet0/1
L          10.10.3.1/32 is directly connected, GigabitEthernet0/1
        172.16.0.0/24 is subnetted, 1 subnets
S          172.16.1.0/24 is directly connected, GigabitEthernet0/0
R       192.168.1.0/24 [120/1] via 10.10.1.2, 00:00:15, GigabitEthernet0/2
S*      0.0.0.0/0 is directly connected, GigabitEthernet0/0
```

Router3(config)#do show running-config
```
Building configuration...

Current configuration : 884 bytes
!
version 15.1
no service timestamps log datetime msec
no service timestamps debug datetime msec
no service password-encryption
!
hostname Router3
!
ip cef
no ipv6 cef
!
interface GigabitEthernet0/0
ip address 10.10.2.1 255.255.255.252
duplex auto
speed auto
!
interface GigabitEthernet0/1
ip address 10.10.3.1 255.255.255.252
duplex auto
speed auto
!
interface GigabitEthernet0/2
ip address 10.10.1.1 255.255.255.252
duplex auto
speed auto
!
interface Vlan1
no ip address
```

```
shutdown
!
router rip
version 2
network 10.0.0.0
no auto-summary
!
ip classless
ip route 0.0.0.0 0.0.0.0 GigabitEthernet0/0
ip route 172.16.1.0 255.255.255.0 GigabitEthernet0/0
!
end
```

EXERCISE #51 – Comprehensive Exercise #6

Background Information: You have configured Router3 to provide DHCP service to hosts on the 192.168.1.0/24 and 10.0.10.0/24 networks. Customers on the 192.168.1.0/24 network are reporting that they are unable to connect to any network resources.

Task: Use the output from the troubleshooting commands provided to identify the configuration error.

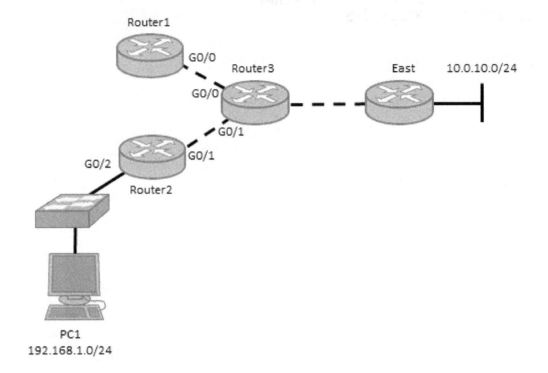

```
Command Prompt – PC1

C:\>ipconfig

IP Address.........................: 169.254.1.112
Subnet Mask.....................: 255.255.0.0
Default Gateway..................:
```

```
Router3(dhcp-config)#do show running-config
Building configuration...

Current configuration : 996 bytes
!
version 15.1
no service timestamps log datetime msec
no service timestamps debug datetime msec
no service password-encryption
!
hostname Router3
```

```
!
ip dhcp pool LEFT
network 192.168.1.0 255.255.255.0
default-router 192.168.1.1
ip dhcp pool RIGHT
network 10.0.10.0 255.255.255.0
default-router 10.0.10.1
!
interface GigabitEthernet0/0
ip address 10.10.2.2 255.255.255.252
duplex auto
speed auto
!
interface GigabitEthernet0/1
ip address 10.10.1.2 255.255.255.252
duplex auto
speed auto
!
interface GigabitEthernet0/2
ip address 10.10.3.2 255.255.255.252
duplex auto
speed auto
!
interface Vlan1
no ip address
shutdown
!
ip route 192.168.1.0 255.255.255.0 GigabitEthernet0/1
ip route 10.0.10.0 255.255.255.0 GigabitEthernet0/2
!
end
```

Router3#show ip dhcp binding

IP address	Client-ID/ Hardware address	Lease expiration	Type
10.0.10.2	FADA.BF18.A763	--	Automatic
10.0.10.3	F133.B007.A123	--	Automatic
10.0.10.4	DDEA.BE23.FDAD	--	Automatic

Router2#show running-config
```
Building configuration...

Current configuration : 789 bytes
!
version 15.1
no service timestamps log datetime msec
no service timestamps debug datetime msec
no service password-encryption
!
hostname Router2
!
```

```
ip cef
no ipv6 cef
!
interface GigabitEthernet0/0
no ip address
duplex auto
speed auto
shutdown
!
interface GigabitEthernet0/1
ip address 10.10.1.1 255.255.255.252
duplex auto
speed auto
!
interface GigabitEthernet0/2
ip address 192.168.1.1 255.255.255.0
duplex auto
speed auto
!
interface Vlan1
no ip address
shutdown
!
ip route 0.0.0.0 0.0.0.0 GigabitEthernet0/1
!
end
```

EXERCISE #52 – Comprehensive Exercise #7

Background Information: Users on your 2001:db8:acac:1000::/64 network cannot connect to the 2001:db8:acac:2000::/64 network. They are able to connect to the 2001:db8:acac:3000::/64 network. You attempt to ping the G0/2 interface of the Eastside router from the 1000::/64 network and note that the ping is successful, but pings to the G0/1 interface of the Eastside router fail.

Task: Use the output from the troubleshooting commands provided to identify the two configuration errors.

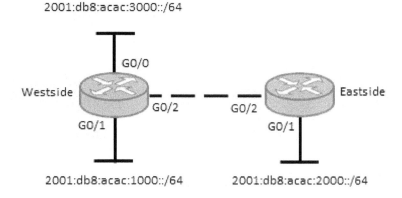

```
Westside(dhcp-config)#do show running-config
Building configuration...

Current configuration : 996 bytes
!
version 15.1
no service timestamps log datetime msec
no service timestamps debug datetime msec
no service password-encryption
!
hostname Westside
!
ipv6 unicast-routing
!
interface GigabitEthernet0/0
no ip address
duplex auto
speed auto
ipv6 address 2001:DB8:ACAC:3000::1/64
!
interface GigabitEthernet0/1
no ip address
duplex auto
speed auto
ipv6 address 2001:DB8:ACAC:1000::1/64
!
interface GigabitEthernet0/2
no ip address
```

```
duplex auto
speed auto
ipv6 address 2001:DB8:ACAC::1/64
!
interface Vlan1
no ip address
shutdown
!
ipv6 route 2001:DB8:ACAC:2000::/64 2001:DB8:ACCC::2
!
end
```

Eastside#show running-config
```
Building configuration...

Current configuration : 996 bytes
!
version 15.1
no service timestamps log datetime msec
no service timestamps debug datetime msec
no service password-encryption
!
hostname Eastside
!
ipv6 unicast-routing
!
interface GigabitEthernet0/0
no ip address
duplex auto
speed auto
!
interface GigabitEthernet0/1
no ip address
duplex auto
speed auto
ipv6 address 2001:DB8:ACAC:2000::1/64
!
interface GigabitEthernet0/2
no ip address
duplex auto
speed auto
ipv6 address 2001:DB8:ACAC::2/64
!
interface Vlan1
no ip address
shutdown
!
end
```

EXERCISE #53 – Comprehensive Exercise #8

Background Information: Your four-router network is having connectivity issues. You have noticed that the subnetworks served by RouterD (2001:db8:afaf:3000/64 and 2001:db8:afaf:4000/64) are able to communicate with each other, as are the networks served by RouterA and RouterB (2001:db8:afaf:1000/64 and 2001:db8:afaf:2000/64). Despite this, you are not seeing end-to-end connectivity across the entire network.

Task: Use the output from the troubleshooting commands provided to identify the configuration error.

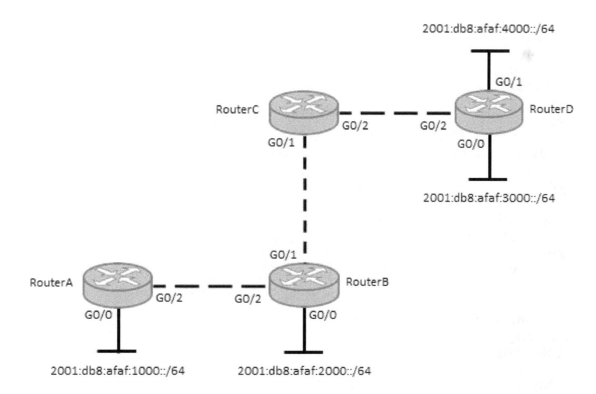

```
RouterD(config)#do show ipv6 interface brief
GigabitEthernet0/0 [up/up]
    FE80::222:97FF:FED5:3701
    2001:DB8:AFAF:3000::1
GigabitEthernet0/1 [up/up]
    FE80::222:97FF:FED5:3702
    2001:DB8:AFAF:4000::1
GigabitEthernet0/2 [up/up]
    FE80::222:97FF:FED5:3703
    2001:DB8:AFAF:3::2


RouterD#ping
Protocol [ip]: ipv6
Target IPv6 address: 2001:db8:afaf:1000::1
Extended commands [n]: y
Source address or interface: 2001:db8:afaf:4000::1
Type escape sequence to abort.
```

```
Sending 5, 100-byte ICMP Echos to 2001:DB8:AFAF:1000::1, timeout is 2
seconds:
Packet sent with a source address of 2001:DB8:AFAF:4000::1
.....
Success rate is 0 percent (0/5)
```

RouterA#ping 2001:db8:afaf:4000::1
```
Type escape sequence to abort.
Sending 5, 100-byte ICMP Echos to 2001:db8:afaf:4000::1, timeout is 2
seconds:
.....
Success rate is 0 percent (0/5)
```

RouterA#show ipv6 route
```
IPv6 Routing Table - 6 entries
S    ::/0 [1/0]
          via 2001:DB8:AFAF:1::2, GigabitEthernet0/2
C    2001:DB8:AFAF:1::/64 [0/0]
          via GigabitEthernet0/2, directly connected
L    2001:DB8:AFAF:1::1/128 [0/0]
          via GigabitEthernet0/2, receive
C    2001:DB8:AFAF:1000::/64 [0/0]
          via GigabitEthernet0/0, directly connected
L    2001:DB8:AFAF:1000::1/128 [0/0]
          via GigabitEthernet0/0, receive
```

RouterC(config)#do show ipv6 route
```
IPv6 Routing Table - 10 entries
S    2001:DB8:AFAF:1::/64 [1/0]
          via 2001:DB8:AFAF:2::1
C    2001:DB8:AFAF:2::/64 [0/0]
          via GigabitEthernet0/1, directly connected
L    2001:DB8:AFAF:2::2/128 [0/0]
          via GigabitEthernet0/1, receive
C    2001:DB8:AFAF:3::/64 [0/0]
          via GigabitEthernet0/2, directly connected
L    2001:DB8:AFAF:3::1/128 [0/0]
          via GigabitEthernet0/2, receive
S    2001:DB8:AFAF:1000::/64 [1/0]
          via 2001:DB8:AFAF:2::1
S    2001:DB8:AFAF:2000::/64 [1/0]
          via 2001:DB8:AFAF:2::1
S    2001:DB8:AFAF:3000::/64 [1/0]
          via 2001:DB8:AFAF:2::1
S    2001:DB8:AFAF:4000::/64 [1/0]
          via 2001:DB8:AFAF:2::1
```

```
RouterB#show ipv6 interface brief
GigabitEthernet0/0 [up/up]
     FE80::222:CFFF:FE80:6C01
     2001:DB8:AFAF:2000::1
GigabitEthernet0/1 [up/up]
     FE80::222:CFFF:FE80:6C02
     2001:DB8:AFAF:2::1
GigabitEthernet0/2 [up/up]
     FE80::222:CFFF:FE80:6C03
     2001:DB8:AFAF:1::2
```

```
RouterB#show ipv6 interface brief
GigabitEthernet0/0 [up/up]
```

EXERCISE #54 – Comprehensive Exercise #9

<u>Background Information</u>: Users on the 10.0.2.0 network are unable to resolve domain names, but they are able to communicate with users on the 10.0.1.0 network. You have verified that users on the 10.0.1.0 network are not having domain name resolution issues.

<u>Task</u>: Use the output from the troubleshooting commands provided to identify the configuration error.

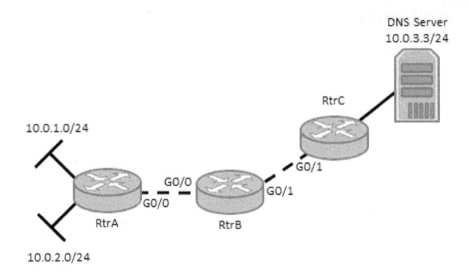

```
RtrC#show ip interface g0/0
GigabitEthernet0/0 is up, line protocol is up (connected)
Internet address is 10.0.3.1/24
Broadcast address is 255.255.255.255
Address determined by setup command
MTU is 1500 bytes
Helper address is not set
Directed broadcast forwarding is disabled
Outgoing access list is not set
Inbound access list is not set
Proxy ARP is enabled
Security level is default
Split horizon is enabled
ICMP redirects are always sent
ICMP unreachables are always sent
ICMP mask replies are never sent


RtrC#show ip interface g0/1
GigabitEthernet0/1 is up, line protocol is up (connected)
Internet address is 10.1.2.2/30
Broadcast address is 255.255.255.255
Address determined by setup command
MTU is 1500 bytes
Helper address is not set
Directed broadcast forwarding is disabled
```

```
Outgoing access list is not set
Inbound access list is 12
Proxy ARP is enabled
Security level is default
Split horizon is enabled
ICMP redirects are always sent
ICMP unreachables are always sent
ICMP mask replies are never sent
```

RtrC#show access-lists
```
Standard IP access list 10
10 permit 10.0.2.0 0.0.0.255

Standard IP access list 12
10 permit 10.0.1.0 0.0.0.255
```

EXERCISE #55 – Comprehensive Exercise #10

<u>Background Information</u>: Employees on the 10.0.2.0/24 network are unable to obtain an IP address from the DHCP router, RtrDHCP. It appears that employees on the 10.0.1.0/24 network can obtain an IP address via DHCP.

<u>Task</u>: Use the output from the troubleshooting commands provided to identify the configuration error.

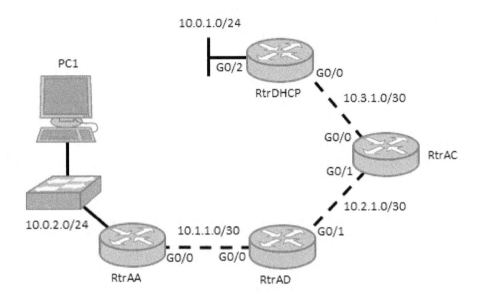

```
RtrDHCP#show ip dhcp pool
Pool North :
Utilization mark (high/low) : 100 / 0
Subnet size (first/next) : 0 / 0
Total addresses : 254
Leased addresses : 1
Excluded addresses : 0
Pending event : none

1 subnet is currently in the pool
Current index     IP address range           Leased/Excluded/Total
10.0.1.1          10.0.1.1 - 10.0.1.254      1 / 0 / 254

Pool South :
Utilization mark (high/low) : 100 / 0
Subnet size (first/next) : 0 / 0
```

```
Total addresses : 254
Leased addresses : 0
Excluded addresses : 0
Pending event : none


1 subnet is currently in the pool
Current index     IP address range          Leased/Excluded/Total
```

RtrDHCP#show running-config | begin ip dhcp
```
ip dhcp pool North
 network 10.0.1.0 255.255.255.0
 default-router 10.0.1.1
ip dhcp pool South
 network 10.0.2.0 255.255.255.0
 default-router 10.0.2.1
!
interface GigabitEthernet0/0
ip address 10.3.1.2 255.255.255.252
duplex auto
speed auto
!
interface GigabitEthernet0/1
no ip address
duplex auto
speed auto
shutdown
!
interface GigabitEthernet0/2
ip address 10.0.1.1 255.255.255.0
duplex auto
speed auto
!
router rip
version 2
network 10.0.0.0
no auto-summary
!
end
```


RtrDHCP#show ip route
```
Gateway of last resort is not set

10.0.0.0/8 is variably subnetted, 5 subnets, 3 masks
C    10.0.1.0/24 is directly connected, GigabitEthernet0/2
L    10.0.1.1/32 is directly connected, GigabitEthernet0/2
R    10.2.1.0/30 [120/1] via 10.3.1.1, 00:00:03, GigabitEthernet0/0
C    10.3.1.0/30 is directly connected, GigabitEthernet0/0
L    10.3.1.2/32 is directly connected, GigabitEthernet0/0
```

RtrAD#show ip route
```
Gateway of last resort is not set

10.0.0.0/8 is variably subnetted, 4 subnets, 2 masks
C 10.1.1.0/30 is directly connected, GigabitEthernet0/0
L 10.1.1.2/32 is directly connected, GigabitEthernet0/0
C 10.2.1.0/30 is directly connected, GigabitEthernet0/1
L 10.2.1.1/32 is directly connected, GigabitEthernet0/1
```

RtrAD#show running-config
```
Building configuration...

Current configuration : 752 bytes
!
version 15.1
no service timestamps log datetime msec
no service timestamps debug datetime msec
no service password-encryption
!
hostname RtrAD
!
ip cef
no ipv6 cef
!
interface GigabitEthernet0/0
ip address 10.1.1.2 255.255.255.252
duplex auto
speed auto
!
interface GigabitEthernet0/1
ip address 10.2.1.1 255.255.255.252
duplex auto
speed auto
!
interface GigabitEthernet0/2
no ip address
duplex auto
speed auto
shutdown
!
router rip
version 2
no auto-summary
!
end
```

RtrAD#show ip protocols

RtrAA#show ip protocols
Routing Protocol is "rip"
Sending updates every 30 seconds, next due in 9 seconds
Invalid after 180 seconds, hold down 180, flushed after 240
Outgoing update filter list for all interfaces is not set
Incoming update filter list for all interfaces is not set
Redistributing: rip
Default version control: send version 2, receive 2
Automatic network summarization is not in effect
Maximum path: 4
Routing for Networks:
     10.0.0.0
Passive Interface(s):
Routing Information Sources:
     Gateway Distance Last Update
Distance: (default is 120)

SOLUTIONS TO EXERCISES FOR CHAPTER 8

SOLUTION - EXERCISE #46

In this exercise, there are three errors that are causing three problems with our network. The first issue is that the Sales VLAN hosts are getting APIPA addresses, which indicates that DHCP cannot connect, either to or from the Buffalo router. A look at the Buffalo router *show running-config* output will confirm that the DHCP pool is configured correctly. The issue is located on the LosAngeles router, specifically on the sub-interface gateway, G0/1.12. You'll notice from that router's *show running-config* output that the interface is missing the *IP helper-address* command, which is used to enable that gateway interface to forward DHCP messages to the Buffalo router. Without that command, DHCP discover messages will not be forwarded and DHCP requests will therefore be unsuccessful.

The second issue is that the Miami branch hosts cannot connect to the network. This is due to an ACL applied to interface G0/1 in the wrong direction. The ACL, which is ACL 99, is set in the inbound direction, which given the way the ACL is written, is blocking all traffic from leaving the network, including any DHCP discover requests. This is due to the implicit deny at the end of the ACL.

The third issue is that the file server does not have connectivity. This is because the gateway interface G0/2 has an address of 10.0.1.1 with a subnet mask of 255.255.255.252, which is a /30 mask and limits the range of that subnet to 10.0.1.1 – 10.0.1.2. This is causing the router to falsely believe that the file server is not located on that LAN segment.

SOLUTION - EXERCISE #47

In this exercise there is only one minor error, which can be seen in both the *show running-config* and the *show ip protocols* commands on Router2. When viewing the output of these commands, take notice that the RIP protocol is configured to advertise the 10.0.1.0 network, but not the 172.16.1.0/24 network. We can see in the *show running-config* and the *show protocols* commands that the interface serving the 172.16.1.0/24 network is up and configured correctly, but it was never entered into the RIP configuration. Because of this error, no other router will learn about the network.

SOLUTION - EXERCISE #48

The only error in this configuration is that the IP addresses for the G0/0 and G0/2 interfaces on Router2 were swapped. This is causing that router to be inconsistent with the static routing commands that it does have, which are correct. Any traffic that does make it to this router that is destined for the user networks would be sent the opposite direction.

SOLUTION - EXERCISE #49

This exercise has a lot of information to sort through, but by looking closely, we can see from the *show interfaces trunk* command that the trunk interface G0/1 is trunked but is not configured to allow traffic tagged as VLAN 11. This will stop any users, including PC2, from communicating out to the router and beyond. The second error is in the server's command output. Notice here that the server has the wrong IP address assigned - 192.168.133.5 instead of 192.168.13.5. This typo places the server on a different subnetwork than its gateway, and since it is misconfigured, it will not respond to pings to the correct IP address.

SOLUTION - EXERCISE #50

This exercise also has a good bit of information to sort through. In this exercise there is only one error, which pertains to the routing on Router3, which is acting like a central hub with all routing passing through it. In the *show ip route* command output on Router3 we can see that the route to the 172.16.1.0/24 network is a static route with an exit interface of G0/0. The *show running-config* output shows the specific error, which is that Router3 has an unneeded static route applied. This static route has a default administrative distance of 1, which therefore supersedes and overrides the routing decisions made by RIP, since RIP has a higher administrative distance of 120.

SOLUTION - EXERCISE #51

This is a challenging exercise related to DHCP, mostly because the error is minor. In this exercise, we see that PC1 is showing us the output from running an *ipconfig* command locally. The address 169.254.1.112 is an APIPA address, which indicates that this host is attempting to secure an IP address from DHCP, but is unable to do so. Next, we see from the *do show running-config* command on Router3 that the interfaces are configured correctly and that DHCP is configured correctly with both LAN pools set up. The *show ip dhcp binding* output shows us that DHCP is functioning correctly for the 10.0.10.0/24 network, but since there are no IP address bindings for the 192.168.1.0/24 network as there should be, we can confirm that something is wrong. We finally see the error in the *show running-config* output on Router2. The gateway interface for the 192.168.1.0/24 network needs to have an IP helper-address, but does not have one in the configuration. The administrator should have entered the *ip helper-address* command on East's 10.0.10.1 interface and pointed it to Router3, to get DHCP requests from that network to Router3.

SOLUTION - EXERCISE #52

This exercise presents another challenging problem due to its simplicity. There are two errors in the configurations. First, the Westside router's static route command is incorrect, as it is set to forward traffic to an IPv6 address that does not exist. Secondly, the Eastside router does not have any route at all to enable it to reach the subnetworks on the Westside router. Since interface G0/2 on the Eastside router is directly connected to the Westside router, you were able to ping that interface, but because of the errors in static routing, you would not be able to reach from subnetwork to subnetwork between the two routers.

SOLUTION - EXERCISE #53

This is another exercise that may prove quite challenging. Here we see that we are using IPv6 and static routing. We also note that the addressing for the point-to-point connections between routers is not defined, but we can determine the addressing based on the command output. In the exercise, there is a single error which is located on RouterC. By viewing the *show ipv6 route* command output on RouterC, we can determine that this router is set up to send all traffic to RouterB's address of 2001:db8:afaf:2::1. This is causing a routing loop in that any traffic being sent to the networks of RouterD is being sent back to RouterB by RouterC, which will in turn send the traffic back to RouterC again.

SOLUTION - EXERCISE #54

This exercise has a standard access control list is that causing an issue with the ability of the 10.0.2.0 network to communicate with the DNS server. Specifically, we can see from the *show ip interface* commands that RtrC has standard ACL number 12 applied in an inbound direction on interface G0/1. From the *show access-lists* command output, we can see that there are two standard access lists, number 10 and 12, and that ACL 12 permits only the 10.0.1.0/24 network. Because it does not explicitly permit the 10.0.2.0 network, that network is caught in the implicit deny that is contained automatically in all access control lists.

SOLUTION - EXERCISE #55

In this exercise, we see that the router RtrDHCP is correctly configured to provide IP addresses for both the 10.0.1.0 and 10.0.2.0 networks. However, note that the router's routing table does not include the 10.0.2.0 network. From the lack of output in RtrAD's *show ip protocols* command, and its *show running-config* command output, we can see that the RIP protocol was installed on the router, but the protocol is not advertising any networks. Because of this, RIP is not functional across the entire network, and therefore the 10.0.2.0 network cannot reach the RtrDHCP router, which is why it cannot acquire a DHCP-issued address.

CHAPTER 9: Other Show Commands To Know

There are a few other show commands that you should expect to see on the CCENT exam that usually have more to do with verification of information than troubleshooting. Make sure that you're familiar with these commands and when you would use them.

show arp

This command shows the address resolution protocol (ARP) table that is currently held in memory on the device. You can use this command as another method for mapping out the topology of the network, or for verifying that devices are able to communicate with each other. This command will show you the IP and MAC addresses of the devices that have been learned and added to the ARP table, but more importantly, it will also show the interfaces that those MAC addresses came in on, providing you with topology information.

show clock

This command displays the current time of the system clock on the device. If you use it with the variant *show clock detail*, you can also learn how the device is acquiring the time. This is a useful command to use in conjunction with anything to do with the Network Time Protocol, or security time verifications related to logging. It is important for security and other network processes that all system times on the network are synced as closely as possible, and the *show clock* command is a way to verify this information.

show controllers

This command displays the status of the interface controllers and hardware. At the CCENT level, the command is used to verify which end of a serial cable is the DTE or DCE end, and what type of cable is connected to an interface. Use the *show controllers* command as a verification of layer 1 wiring.

show file systems

The *show file systems* command displays the total storage space and free space available on the device. Use this command in coordination with the *show flash:* command, for example, to see what files are specifically located in the storage.

show flash:

This command shows information about the flash storage on the device, including the files that it contains. Use this command in coordination with the *show file systems* command to see total storage and free space for flash storage, as well as view the IOS image and vlan.dat file stored in flash.

show history

The *show history* command provides the history of the commands entered into the device. This is very useful to see what another user has done or attempted to do on a device in the recent past. On most devices, the history is set by default to hold the last ten entries, but the amount can be adjusted by applying *the history size number* command in the line configuration menu. You can also scroll through the history by using the up and down arrows.

show license / show license feature / show license udi

These commands show the licensing information of your device. The UDI option shows the product ID of your device, as well as the Unique Device Identifier (UDI) and serial number. The feature option shows the features available on your device. These features are often used to verify warranty and licensing information.

show ntp status / show ntp associations

These commands show the Network Time Protocol status and any associations it has developed with other devices that the protocol can connect with on the network. Use these commands in coordination with the *show clock* command to verify the system time and NTP functionality. Closely synchronized timestamps between devices on a network becomes highly important for logging and security, and the Network Time Protocol is designed to ensure that this occurs.

show users

The *show users* command shows any active connections currently on the terminal lines. Use this command in coordination with the *show ssh* command to verify connections inbound and outbound via SSH.

show version

This command shows the current IOS version running on the device and provides hardware and software information about the system. The *show version* command also provides the current configuration register setting, which is useful for password resets, if necessary. Use this command to verify the IOS version on a device, and in turn whether that specific IOS version is compatible with specific features, such as IPv6 routing.

Conclusion

I hope you've enjoyed this book and the process of working through the troubleshooting exercises contained inside. A great deal of consideration and care went into their crafting to provide you with a solid opportunity for building and improving your troubleshooting skill set and preparing for the certification exam. I wish you the best in your career and certification efforts!

www.ingramcontent.com/pod-product-compliance
Lightning Source LLC
Chambersburg PA
CBHW060133060326

40690CB00018B/3859